CLAYWORK Form and Idea in Ceramic Design

CLAYWORK

Form and Idea in Ceramic Design

Leon I. Nigrosh

Co-published in Texas by
Hendrick-Long Publishing Company, Dallas, Texas
and Davis Publications, Inc., Worcester, Massachusetts

Photography by **Bill Byers**
Drawings by **Donald Krueger**

Printed in the United States of America
Library of Congress Catalog Card Number: 74-31687
ISBN 0-87192-069-7

Printing: The Alpine Press
Type: Newton (Helvetica), set by Computer Graphics Corp
Design: Jane Pitts

Consulting Editors: George F. Horn and Sarita R. Rainey

10 9 8 7 6 5

Preface

A good friend once asked me how it felt to be useless. He was amazed that I was working clay by hand in the second half of the twentieth century. Machines today have taken over, providing the populace with all the ceramic dishes, lamps, ashtrays, and doorknobs it will ever need, and more. The studio potter using ancient time-consuming methods is no match for modern industry. In reaction, some clayworkers have rejected the entire ten thousand year heritage of clay to make either nonfunctional decorative objects or disfunctional objects, such as teapots that do not work, as propaganda diatribes against their supposed lost stature in the community.

However, within our society there is, or can be, an important place for a person who makes things of clay. A sensitive clayworker can create objects of simplicity, beauty, and life to fill a growing need for the human touch in our steadily depersonalizing existence.

Working in clay is also self-satisfying. From the inception of an idea through the actual shaping of the material, choosing the color and controlling the fire, one is in total personal command of the project. The success is all due to you—but so too is failure. A harmony is developed between yourself and nature, for no matter how adept you become with the skills of working in clay, natural forces always loom to either assist or resist those labors. You must have feeling for the material and understand it thoroughly in order to draw anything of value from it. To make a clay bowl is one thing; to make that bowl a work of art is quite another.

This book is for beginners as well as for those with experience who want to make art of clay. Conceived as a basic studio course, it is also an up-to-date reference presenting many examples of contemporary American clayworks. It explores ceramics from its beginning to the present. Photographs taken especially for this book show time-honored forming methods along with modern time-saving ways to accomplish similar results. Of particular importance, the book provides picture sequences photographed as if the reader were actually performing the operation. Not only are the traditional decorating techniques described, but included for the first time are discussions of recent experimentation with decal methods and photo imagery on clay.

Principles of ceramic design, often overlooked in other books, are offered here to help the reader increase the aesthetic value of his or her clay objects. And a chapter on the basics of marketing explains how to get started selling ware and how to receive a fair market price for it.

The technical side of ceramics often frightens newcomers to clay and some old hands as well. Clayworkers have especially been uneasy visitors to the chemistry laboratory. It is reassuring to know that a number of chemical components do not pertain to the glaze process. To bring the necessary information to the studio, all the chemical formulas in this book have been separated into the essential oxide relationships instead of the usual more complex chemists' formulas. A detailed discussion of the properties of each raw material used in glaze formulation has been included in the appendix along with element formula weight charts.

To help translate concept into reality and creative idea into created form, every effort has been made to present a concise explanation of the many aspects of claywork.

Acknowledgments

Many people deserve thanks for helping me to write the book, including all of those clayworkers who submitted photos for consideration, and especially those who are represented in these pages. Specifically, I wish to thank James Winegar for allowing me to publish his kiln building plans and both Gerry Williams and Victor Spinski for their help in presenting the information on photo resist. Ceramic engineer O. Mason Burrows performed an inestimable service in helping to clarify the mysteries of glaze formulation. A word of thanks is due Howard Kottler for his provocative, if not cynical, questions as to the need for another ceramic book, which kept things in focus, I hope. The critical comments by Angelo Garzio from the artist-teacher's viewpoint and those of my friend and student Linda Freedman were valuable guideposts in the refining of the manuscript. The staff of Davis Publications deserves a note of appreciation for their assistance in developing and designing this volume. I am most grateful to my wife, Gale, who took time off from her own work to give me encouragement and editorial assistance.

L. I. N.

Contents

Introduction

Clay appeared on earth long before living beings. It was therefore inevitable that humans would eventually begin to examine and to apply their imagination to the abundant amorphous material. From these early tactile ventures, a rich panoply of objects, both crude and refined, has continued to be created, evidencing the strides that humankind has made over tens of thousands of years. In many instances, the only remaining evidence of bygone civilizations is fired clay objects unearthed in archaeological digs. These broken pieces of clay provide the barest hints of the growth and decline of many peoples. Moreover, a curious similarity has been noted in the shape and decoration of some objects from cultures separated by thousands of miles and many centuries. If enough clayworks can be found, maybe the true story of humanity will someday be known.

Because soft clay can be easily modeled into any shape and then fired to permanency, it continues to be used as both a form of expression and a practical convenience. During the Neolithic Age, ten or twelve thousand years ago, the growth of agrarian civilization produced an ever increasing demand for storage containers and cooking utensils, which were often carved stone vessels and woven hemp baskets. Unfortunately, the former were laborious to make and the latter had a short life span. To make baskets more durable and waterproof, people lined them with mud; but, eventually, these baskets rotted and new ones had to be made. At some point a useless basket was probably cast on an open fire, and later, in the smoldering ashes, small hard pieces of clay were found. This became the way pots were first made—by pressing clay into baskets which were then burned away. Crosshatched indentations on the surface of ancient shards now displayed in many museums serve as evidence to support this theory. Even after other forming methods came into use, the crosshatch design persisted as an important decorative motif in many cultures.

Fertility fetishes provide other examples of early clayworks. Crudely formed and hardened by simply being thrown into a fire, these objects have survived the centuries to serve as mute reminders of the human capacity for creativity and the desire for self perpetuation.

Pottery forms also had an important part in burial ceremonies. Often, as in pre-Columbian South America, death masks or portrait urns were made either to mollify the gods or store the souls of the departed.

1 Prehistoric Vase
Earthenware, slip decoration
Ragy, Iran
Polished earthenware, black paint
6 x 7 inches
Courtesy: Museum of Fine Arts, Boston
    University Museum Fund

2 Fertility Figure
Earthenware
Predynastic Egypt
7 inches high
Courtesy: Museum of Fine Arts, Boston
    Sears Fund

3 Portrait Urn
Painted earthenware
Pre-Columbian Mexico
16 7/8 x 8 x 9 inches
Courtesy: Worcester Art Museum

4 Nigerian Potter, Ladi Kwali
Coil built vase
24 inches high
Photo: Dr. Robert Englund

3

4

The evolution of ceramic techniques moved from simple hand forming methods through coil building and slab forming and culminated in the discovery and use of the potter's wheel. Many cultures never attained the sophistication of the wheel and others, even today, still rely chiefly on coil building for all their work.

Ceramics eventually fell under the spell of mass production and industrialization. At first, care was still taken to insure the integrity of each ceramic object. However, as the needs of the western world grew and greater numbers meant greater profit, the quality of ceramic design and execution began to deteriorate. Clayworkers attempted to adapt their products to changing life-styles in each society. Inevitably a level of demand was reached where only machinery could meet the needs of the public, and the individual potter was unable to compete economically with the machine. However, the world over, some studio potters continued to work, providing personalized utilitarian objects, but their influence on society as a whole remained at a low ebb for years. It was really not until after the Second World War, that interest in the creating and collecting of claywork was actively renewed in this country. The advent of inexpensive electric kilns for home studios also helped push ceramics back into the public eye.

The growth of interest in ceramics here and subsequently abroad has been due primarily to a return to humanistic concerns. Weary of the glass and steel monoliths that overspread our landscape, we are returning to the earth in a variety of ways. Home gardening, home sewing—the do-it-yourself ethos—are all individual expressions in reaction to the products of a mass society. What more obvious a medium with which to express oneself than that abundant, amorphous material that so fascinated ancient people. We have come full circle, returning to civilization's earliest experiments in creativity—clay.

10

5 *Rape of the Sabines*
18th century Austrian
Cast porcelain
13 1/2 inches high
Courtesy: Museum of Fine Arts, Boston
  Gift of Mrs. T. O. Richardson

6 Bernard Leach
Thrown stoneware pitcher and vase
left: 13 1/2 inches high;
right: 8 1/2 inches high
Courtesy: Colby College Art Museum

7 Henry Varnum Poor
Thrown stoneware pitcher, plate and jug
Pitcher: 8 inch high
Plate: 8 inches diameter
Jug: 6 3/4 inches high
Courtesy: Colby College Art Museum

6

5

7

1-1

1-1 Larry Oughton
Aurora
Molded porcelain, fur and plexiglas
24 inch diameter

CHAPTER 1 Clay

How Clay is Formed

The earth was once a mass of molten material. As the planet cooled, the heavier materials began to settle into relatively distinct layers. The surface layer formed by this cooling is made up of what is known as igneous rock. This cooled molten rock consists of almost 60 percent silica and about 15 percent alumina, both important elements in the ceramic process. Eons ago, water, wind, ice, and the expansions and contractions of the planet began to pulverize the rock, depositing silica and alumina particles along with other minerals and organic matter all over the globe. The resulting conglomerate is clay. Every day, new clay is being formed by the decomposition of rock while at the same time new rock is being formed by natural heat and pressure fusion of clay. The chemical formula for clay in its unfired state is:

$$Al_2O_3 \cdot 2SiO_2 \cdot 2H_2O$$

This formula of one molecule of alumina to two molecules of silica and two of water is an ideal one which does not take into consideration the many metal oxides and organic matter found in clay. Localized variations and amounts of these additional materials account for the different types of clay deposits found on the surface of the earth.

Primary, or residual clays, are those which remain in the site where they were formed. Secondary, or sedimentary, clays have been transported by water, wind or glacier from their original site. Primary clays are characterized by their coarse grain, high refractory or heat resistant quality, low plasticity, and their whiter fired color. All of these characteristics are due to the fact that the clays have not been moved and have few, if any, impurities. As secondary clays are transported farther away from their parent site, they become naturally more finely ground and contaminated with organic matter and minerals. Because of this, the clays are less refractory, more plastic, and fire from tan to brown or black.

Types of Clay

Clays may be broadly classified in descending order of purity in relation to the ideal chemical formula, and they are described in that order here.

Kaolins or China Clays are white firing, highly refractory, relatively nonplastic primary clays. Scattered deposits of kaolin exist in Europe, North America, England and Asia, but not to the extent of other types of clay. Kaolins are highly regarded for their purity, or lack of contamination, and are essential in the production of chinaware, porcelain, and many industrial ceramics. Kaolins have a melting point above 1800°C (3272°F) and poor plasticity because of their coarse grain structure. To improve workability and lower the maturing temperature, other clays and materials are often used in combination with kaolins. Because kaolins are pure clays, they provide a good source for alumina and silica in glazes.

Stoneware Clays are secondary clays which fire from buff to brown or grey, are refractory and, generally, fairly plastic. The fired color and maturing temperature of stonewares depend upon the amount and kind of impurities such as iron, feldspar or calcium which might be present in the deposit. Stoneware clays are often used by studio potters because they are easy to handle, and have a long firing range, between 1177° and 1306°C (2151° - 2383°F), and good vitrification, or hardness, when fired. Although some stonewares can be used alone for throwing or forming, mixtures of stoneware and other clays and materials are often used for improved workability, texture and color.

Fireclays may vary greatly in color and plasticity, but they all have a high resistance to heat. Because of this quality, fireclays are used to make firebricks for kilns and furnaces, kiln furniture and other refractory parts for boilers and smelters, as well as insulating brick. Fireclays are often mixed with stoneware clays to increase refractoriness, improve texture, and give interesting variations in color.

Earthenware Clays are highly contaminated with iron oxide and, therefore, generally fire red to black. Because of large amounts of impurities, earthenware clays do not become vitreous when fired and often begin to melt at temperatures about 1050°C (1922°F). The plasticity of earthenware can vary from sticky to grainy nonplastic, depending on the location of the deposit. Some clays are unusable because they contain mineral fragments which might explode or soluble salts which cause scumming and discoloration. Many outcroppings can be made usable with minor alterations such as washing away salts or adding other clays.

Terra cotta is a type of coarse grained nonvitreous earthenware which is most often used for sculpture.

1-2 Pat Lay
Slab-built and thrown stoneware
sculpture
48 inches high

1-3

1-3 Judy Rose Dornbush
Garden Earth
Handbuilt and molded earthenware
12 inches high
Collection: Mr. & Mrs. Rodney Blasche

Ball Clays are sedimentary clays found near coal deposits or in swamp areas. Because they are contaminated chiefly by organic matter, ball clays are quite plastic. The fine grain size of the clay imparts a high shrinkage rate of some 20 percent and makes it difficult to use by itself. However, a combination of coarse-grained, less plastic kaolin and ball clay often makes a workable, high-firing white clay body. When used in conjunction with other clays, ball clays impart increased plasticity, improved dry strength, and better vitrification.

Surface Clays such as adobe are nonplastic, sandy, and suitable mainly for making sun-dried brick. Shale can be pulverized, water-soaked for a long period of time and then used for the manufacture of brick, roof, and drain tile and other rough clay products. Soil clays, sometimes called Gumbos, are usually too contaminated and sticky to be very useful.

Slip Clays naturally contain enough fluxing agents, such as feldspar and certain alkolins, to perform as glazes when fired above 1201°C (2194°F). Although there are some white firing slip clays, most fire tan to black, as do Albany Slip Clay and Barnard Clay.

Bentonite is a fine particled volcanic ash clay which can be used in small amounts as a plasticizer in clay bodies. Bentonite will also act as a floatative in glazes when used in amounts of 3 percent or less. In either case, it is best to dry mix all the ingredients before adding water because bentonite tends to gum up if added to a watery solution, forming little clumps in the clay or glaze.

Clay Bodies

It is possible to work with many clays just as they come from the ground. Often, however, they do not possess certain desired characteristics such as color, plasticity, strength, or fired density. By mixing two or more clays and adding other materials, these effects can be produced in what is called a clay body. In order to do this intelligently, it is first necessary to know the physical properties of the materials to be used.

Tests for Clay

When choosing a clay with which to work, three important qualities should first be determined: plasticity, shrinkage, and porosity.

1-4

Plasticity is that quality of clay necessary for good work-ability. If a clay is too plastic or sticky, it will not handle easily. If it is less plastic, or short, the clay will not take much stress when it is used.

To determine the amount of water needed to make a clay plastic, weigh one hundred grams of powdered dry clay. Fill a 100 cubic centimeter (cc.) graduated cylinder with water. Slowly mix the water into the dry powder until the clay has developed a plastic quality. First record the amount of water used to make the clay plastic and then the additional amount necessary to develop stickiness. This will give the range of water content in which the clay is workable. The cubic centimeters of water equal the percentage of water of plasticity (1 cc. of water weighs 1 gram).

A simple test for plasticity is to roll a pencil-thick coil of clay and wrap it around a finger. If the coil cracks, the clay is short and will not work well.

Aging the clay will improve its plasticity. Clay which has been moistened, well mixed, and stored for at least three weeks (the Chinese aged clay for whole generations!) will have improved plasticity. This is due to a chemical break-down caused by organic matter contained in the clay. A small amount of vinegar added to the water in the clay will help induce decomposition. Plasticizers such as bentonite or commercial chemicals can be helpful, but should be used sparingly.

Kneading the clay thoroughly before use aligns clay particles and will improve plasticity.

To decrease plasticity, less plastic or nonplastic fillers, such as grog (prefired clay), sand, or organic materials like sawdust, can be added.

Shrinkage occurs in stages. The initial shrinking of the clay takes place when it dries as water evaporates. Additional shrinkage happens in the bisque, or first, firing when the chemically combined water is driven out. Further shrinkage occurs in the upper heat ranges when chemical compounds in the clay begin to fuse.

To test for shrinkage, make a number of clay bars, 13 centimeters long, 4 cm. wide and 1 cm. thick. A line 10 cm. long is drawn on the face of each bar. Allow the bars to dry, and as they do, either sandwich them between newspaper and light boards above and below or turn them over frequently to avoid warping. When dry, measure the line and determine the dry shrinkage by the following calculation:

$$\frac{\text{Wet Length - Dry Length}}{\text{Wet Length}} \times 100 = \text{Percent Dry Shrinkage}$$

This formula states, for example, that if the dry length of the bar is 8.5 cm., that number is subtracted from the wet length of 10 cm. leaving 1.5 cm. This is divided by the wet length 10 cm., giving the number .15 which is multiplied by 100 to show a dry shrinkage of 15 percent.

For those whose minds go numb at the sign of a mathematical forumula, there is an easier way to measure shrinkage. Using a centimeter ruler, simply count back from 10 cm. to the actual dry measurement. The number of millimeters the bar has shrunk equals the percent dry shrinkage.

Next, the bars are fired to temperature and the lines measured again. The fired shrinkage is then calculated:

$$\frac{\text{Dry Length - Fired Length}}{\text{Dry Length}} \times 100 = \text{Percent Fired Shrinkage}$$

The total shrinkage is the sum of the Percent Dry and Fired Shrinkages.

Natural shrinkages can vary from 10 to 25 percent, with a rate of between 12 to 15 percent considered good. Clay bodies can be formulated to have zero shrinkage or even be made to expand slightly when fired. This is most often done only for exacting industrial and scientific items.

Porosity is the measure of maturity of a fired clay. The more vitrified the clay, the less water it will absorb. To test for porosity, first weigh unglazed fired samples of the clay. Then soak the samples in water overnight or boil them in water for two hours. Blot the samples immediately after withdrawing them from the water and weigh them again. The absorption is calculated as follows:

$$\frac{\text{Saturated Weight - Dry Weight}}{\text{Dry Weight}} \times 100 = \text{Percentage Absorption}$$

1-7

allows greater freedom for design concept without measurably adding to the cost of raw materials.

A minimum batch of 500 grams of the claybody ingredients is dry mixed. Because most casting slips require only about 35 to 50 percent by weight of water, start by measuring 300 grams of water into a clean bowl. Slowly mix in the dry clay until the slip thickens. At this point, add 0.25 grams of soda ash along with 0.25 cc. of sodium silicate. (Note: 1 cc. sodium silicate weighs 1.3 grams) The slip should then become fluid. Dry clay, deflocculants, and more water are added by measure in this manner until all the clay has been mixed. Record the amounts of water and deflocculants used in the test to determine percentages needed for a larger batch. If the amount of water is much above 50 percent, the slip will probably not be satisfactory because of its high rate of shrinkage.

A simple test for fluidity is to stick a hand into the slip, withdraw it and spread the fingers apart. If the slip momentarily "webs" and then drains off smoothly, it is the proper consistency for casting. If the slip is too thick, stir in small amounts of water until the correct consistency is reached. If it is too thin, add more dry clay. Draining off water will draw away the deflocculants. The best test for quality is to pour the slip into a mold and note how well it builds up against the sides and how well it drains. The stiffened slip should easily come away from the mold and then dry with minimum warpage.

Larger batches of slip should be mixed thoroughly by hand or clay blunger and passed through a 60- to 80-mesh screen before use. Slip should be stored in airtight containers.

Dry casting scraps can be added to new batches of slip. This can possibly upset the delicate balance of deflocculant, so additions should remain under 10 percent of the total batch.

It is important to note that sodium silicate left to dry in the glass graduate will solidify and thicken the walls, giving inaccurate later readings. To prevent this, wash the glass with vinegar immediately after using.

Preparing Clay for Use

It is important to emphasize again that clay that is too soft or too stiff and filled with hard chunks or air bubbles is difficult to use. For best results, clay should be de-aired and have an even consistency.

Two basic methods for preparing clay are used worldwide. One is the Western method, called *wedging*; the other is the Far Eastern way, *kneading*. To wedge, a convenient amount of clay is first patted into a cube. **1-8,** The cube is then sliced diagonally in half, using a wire. Holding a wedge in each hand, first one portion is raised overhead and slammed down on the board and then the other is slammed on top of the first, just slightly behind the closest edge, forcing air out of the clay. **1-9,** This lump is then sliced diagonally again and the procedure is repeated ten to twenty times until the clay is thoroughly mixed. If improperly done, air bubbles will remain in the cube, making it difficult to use. The major drawback to this method is that the physical strength required to lift the wedges overhead limits the amount of clay that can be prepared at one time. Other minor drawbacks are the noise and the possible "shotgunning" of wet clay bits around the studio caused by slamming the clay.

Kneading has many advantages over wedging. Greater amounts of clay can be processed at one time, it is quieter and, because the whole body comes into action, does not require as much effort. This method can best be executed on a sturdy canvas-covered table, 30 to 32 inches high, or by kneeling on the floor. **1-10,** A ball of clay is first pushed out of round firmly with the palms of both hands, keeping the arms straight and using the shoulders and back to exert pressure. With either hand, lift the far end of the clay and raise it forward over the leading edge with a quarter twist. Push

1-8

1-9

1-10

1-11

1-12

down and away with both hands. Repeat this procedure using the same hand to lift each time. **1-11,** A rhythmic rocking motion of the body will be created which will facilitate this operation. **1-12,** The quarter twist motion shapes the clay into a spiral, or cornucopia, exposing an everchanging clay surface which allows air bubbles to break out at the base while thoroughly mixing the clay. If the clay is only rolled, air will remain trapped inside. Continue to knead in this manner at least 15 or 20 times to insure full homogenization. There is

no need to slice the clay to check for consistency if the process is well executed. Slicing is more often counter-productive in that it makes more air pockets which must then be kneaded out when the pieces are recombined.

If the clay is too soft for use, continue to knead. If the clay is quite stiff, cut the ball into thin slices and alternate them with layers of thick slurry to form a "Dagwood sandwich." Then knead everything together until the clay is plastic and workable.

CHAPTER 2 **Pinch**

The pinch method was the first method to use only the potter's hands to shape the clay. By inserting the thumb of one hand into a ball of clay and lightly pinching with thumb and fingers while slowly rotating the ball in the palm of the other hand, a small pot can be rapidly made.

2-1

2-3

2-2

21

2-7 Raku Teabowls
19th Century Japanese Yamashiro ware
left: 4 1/2 inch diameter:
right: 4 inch diameter
Courtesy: Museum of Art, Rhode Island
   School of Design, Providence, R.I.
   Gift of Isaac C. Bates

2-8 Nancy Selvage
Raku Form
12 x 6 inches

2-4

2-5

2-6

2-7

2-8

2-9 Harriet Taub
Pinch-formed stoneware bottles
left: 7 inches high; right: 4 inches high

2-9

2-10

2-11

2-12

2-13

If cracks appear in the clay because the pinching is drying it too fast, do not smear water on the clay, but simply moisten the fingertips by pressing on a damp sponge. If the clay is too soft and the form starts to flop about, put the piece aside until it stiffens and work on another shape while waiting.

Instead of forcing this method to make some pre-established form, work *with* the clay, not against it. Experiment with the size of the ball and the way the fingers are held in relation to the thumb. Can tall thin pots be made? How wide can a form be shaped? By freeing the mind of preconceived ideas and working with the clay, simple elegant shapes can be created in the same manner ancient raku teabowls were formed.

With imagination many different objects can be made although the pinch technique itself may be limiting. **2-10,** Using two hemispheres joined securely lip to lip, a pot can be made twice as big. **2-14,** A smaller pot sealed bottom to bottom with a larger one can produce a footed form. Clusters of small pinch pots can be made into cactus planters or sculptures.

2-14

2-15

2-16

2-17

2-18 Don McCance
Pinch-formed stoneware goblets,
   luster glaze
6 x 3 inches

2-19 Nadine Hurst
Pinch-formed pot
Unglazed, burnished, sawdust fired
4 1/2 x 6 inches

The textures that can be devised using only the fingers or simple tools are almost limitless.

Another method for making pinch pots, used by some American Indians, is to pat the clay ball against the elbow to form larger, wide-mouthed pots. Other methods using sticks, fists, and so on have often been suggested for making larger pinch pots. Obviously, there is a practical limit to size and larger pots can best be made with other techniques.

Simple cup forms may be placed upside down on the lip to equalize the drying. More complex joined pieces should be covered with lightweight plastic and allowed to set slowly so that they will not come apart from having been dried too rapidly.

Pots should be made with thin, even walls. As clay is fired, the chemically combined water turns to steam. If the clay is too thick, the steam cannot escape rapidly enough, pressure builds up, and the pot will explode.

2-18

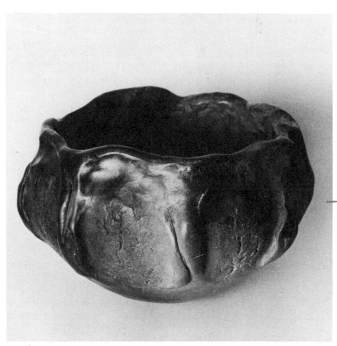

2-19

CHAPTER 3 Coil Building

3-1

3-2 Lekythos
Greek, 470-460 B.C.
Red slip on black earthenware
15 inches high
Courtesy: Wadsworth Atheneum, Hartford

For centuries coil building has been the primary method of making pottery. It still holds that position in some cultures today even though the introduction of the potter's wheel has rendered traditional coil techniques virtually obsolete. In contemporary ceramics the coil method can be used to best advantage, contrary to some current thought, by placing less emphasis on total symmetry in favor of asymmetrical forms. **3-1,** Instead of using templates or other aids to make perfectly round objects as did the Greeks and others, organic forms seem more reasonable to attempt.

The technique of making organic forms is fairly simple. Start by flattening and forming a piece of kneaded clay into the shape desired for a base. The thickness of the base can range from 3/8 to 3/4 of an inch depending on the proposed size of the finished object. **3-3,** The base should be placed on a plaster bat or wood slab on top of a bench wheel, if available, for ease in building.

3-4, To make a coil, squeeze out a long rope of well kneaded clay by hand. The more symmetrical the rope, the easier it will be to roll. **3-5,** Lay this on a table and roll it back and forth, applying light even pressure, keeping hands parallel with the table, and using the full length of the fingers and palms. Short, quick rolling with only fingertips or palms will result in flat, uneven coils. Rolling from the center out or from the ends to the center of the coil makes no difference as long as it is done evenly. There is no real saving in rolling a number of coils before use. The time taken to make each coil

can actually assist in construction, allowing a slight stiffening of the form as the work progresses.

3-6, Flatten one end of the first coil, then press it firmly all around the top of the base until the other end slightly overlaps. **3-7,** Seal the entire inside seam vertically using a finger or wooden tool. Then evenly smooth away all the sealing marks. It is important that this first coil be placed directly on top of the base. Otherwise the piece may come apart in drying or firing.

Each succeeding coil snould be squeezed and rolled in the same manner and firmly attached to the preceding one. **3-8,** Joining the coils smoothly on the inside helps insure against drying cracks, and provides visual contrast to a textured exterior. It also makes the interior easier to clean, which is an important design feature in utilitarian objects.

3-3

3-4

3-5

3-6

3-7

3-8

3-9

3-10

3-11

Textures can be made by fingers, tools, stamping, paddling, and other means. The coils themselves can be used as built-in decorative surfaces by making swirls, holes, bumps, or by varying the height of the coils.

If a smooth surface is sought, or larger forms are desired, a wider coil can be used. To make a wide coil, squeeze and roll out a thick coil and then flatten it. The height of the coil is thus increased while keeping a thin width.

3-11 Mary Jane Edwards
Clay Forms
Coilbuilt stoneware, transparent stains
L to R: 13 x 5, 10 x 5, 15 x 5 inches

3-12 Gary Smith
Coilbuilt stoneware vase
18 x 12 inches

3-13 Gail Seavey
Coilbuilt porcelain sculpture
22 x 8 x 8 inches

3-12

3-13

3-14, Coils can also be made by first rolling a thick slab of clay and then cutting it into strips with either a knife or loop tool. This gives a sharper exposed edge to the coils when they are used.

3-14

3-15

3-16

3-17

3-18 Edward Harkness
Minerva
Coilbuilt and thrown stoneware, salt glaze
31 inches high
Photo: Michael Tylick

3-19

3-20

3-19, To build a bulging form, each coil is placed toward the outer edge of the coil below. To constrict a form, coils are placed toward the inner edge of those underneath.

It is often better to work on more than one object at a time. As coil forms grow, they tend to become quite wobbly and adding more coils could cause collapse. Momentum is not lost, however, if work is continued on a second piece while the first is allowed to set up.

After some initial experimentation with coil rolling, building, and texturing, sketching is suggested before larger or more complex forms are attempted. Sometimes forms can best be built in sections which are assembled after having stiffened. Spouts, pedestals, or other appendages should be made separately and added to the basic form after setting up, instead of trying to build from the bottom up and inviting untimely collapse.

CHAPTER 4 Slab Construction

There are a few methods of making clay slabs, the most obvious of which is to pound the clay flat by hand. Another method, preferred by Far Eastern potters, calls for a wire stretched tightly between two upright sticks cut with a series of equidistant notches. **4-1,** The wire in the bottom notch is pulled through a squared block of clay and then raised a notch for each successive pass.

The easiest way to make slabs of any size is known as the "pizza method." **4-2,** After kneading the clay thoroughly, flatten it slightly by patting. **4-3,** Lift it up by the farthest edge and, without letting go, throw it down against a tabletop or floor with a pulling motion, allowing the far end of the clay to hit first. **4-4,** Repeat the process by grasping the far edge, lifting, slamming the clay down away from the body, and pulling back with a swinging motion until the slab is stretched slightly thicker than the desired thickness. Alternate this action by picking up the slab by a side edge and slapping it down. In this way a relatively squared slab can be made with little effort. If a larger slab is required, two or more small slabs can be joined by welding the edges together until the desired size is obtained.

4-1

4-2

4-3

4-4

4-5 Richard Shaw
Gray Jar w/ Butterflies
Slab-built earthenware, underglaze
18 x 18 inches
Courtesy: Quay Gallery

The slabs are then placed on the floor on top of canvas, burlap or other textured material. Parallel guide sticks, such as two yardsticks, are positioned on either side of, but not touching, the clay. The clay is covered with canvas and a large rolling pin or metal pipe is placed on top of the center of the slab resting firmly on the guide sticks. Stand on the pipe and roll evenly to one end. Replace the pipe in the center and roll to the other end. This method, utilizing body weight, is less tiring than the conventional way of pushing the pipe by hand. If there are ripples in the clay after the first rolling, peel off the top layer of the cloth and turn the clay over onto it. Remove what was the bottom cloth to allow free movement of the clay, set the guide sticks, replace the cloth and roll again.

The thickness of the guide sticks depends on the size of the object to be constructed. Most slab objects can be built within a range of 3/16 inch to 3/4 inch wall thickness. Thicker slabs do not necessarily make stronger pots. In fact, if clay walls are too thick they can hamper the natural drying and firing processes, causing strains and possible splitting.

When making large slabs for wall panels or murals, lay out the clay in workable widths with spaces between for the guide sticks. Fill in these spaces after rolling.

To minimize deformation after the slab is rolled, peel off the top cloth, turn the clay over onto it and remove the bottom cloth before any cutting is done. At this time the pieces are cut to size, using a potter's knife or a pizza cutter. If a flat-sided object is to be made, the pieces should be left to stiffen without moving them. If, however, the slabs must be stored, stack them one on top of another, alternating several sheets of newspaper with each slab. The paper will absorb moisture from the clay and aid in slow, even drying. Wrap the stack in plastic and place the package on a board so that it may be moved without bending the slabs.

4-6 Rick Knopf
Slab-built stoneware bottle,
  horseshoe nails
15 x 5 inches

4-8 George Wolfkeil, ca. 1800
Hard Times in Jersey
Slab-built earthenware dish,
  slip decoration
12 1/4 x 15 5/8 inches
Courtesy: Wadsworth Atheneum, Hartford
Photo: E. Irving Blomstrann

4-9 Arretine Bowl
Merrimac Pottery Company, ca. 1910
Unglazed earthenware
7 1/2 inch diameter
Courtesy: Worcester Art Museum

4-6

Texture can be readily achieved in slab building by rolling out the clay on highly articulated fabrics, such as shag rugs, thermal blankets, burlap, canvas, netting, and even lace. Other surfaces can be created by lightly beating the slab with rope-wrapped or carved paddles, meat tenderizers, broken branches, or whatever the imagination can conceive. The contrast of smooth and rough surfaces on simple slab forms can turn an ordinary pot into something more aesthetically interesting.

4-7, Simple plates or trays can be formed from a freshly rolled and cut slab by turning up and smoothing the edges.

4-7

4-8

4-9

4-10

4-11

4-10, Shallow baking tins or plates can be used as press molds, by first lining them with strips of newspaper to prevent the clay from sticking. Soft slabs can be laid into shallow plaster press molds or over plaster drape molds. 4-12, Feet and handles can be added when the clay has stiffened.

4-12

4-13

4-14

4-15

4-14, Two molded slabs can be joined to form the body of a larger object. Score the edges with a toothed scraper or hacksaw blade, soften them with vinegar and seal firmly together, using thin coils to fill the seams if needed. **4-15,** Spouts, handles, or other appendages can be added for interest as well as function.

Cardboard mailing tubes can be used to form cylindrical objects. Wrap the tube with newspaper to prevent the clay from sticking. **4-16,** Roll a soft slab around the tube and press the edges together, perhaps leaving finger marks as the decoration. For a smooth cylinder, bevel the edges before joining. **4-17,** Stand the tube upright on a clay slab and cut around the tube to make a base. Weld the base to the cylinder. After a short time to allow some stiffening of the clay, remove the cardboard and paper. Clay shrinkage will make later removal very difficult. Seal the interior seams. Finish the top of the clay cylinder by smoothing, tearing, or cutting.

To cap the cylinder, simply invert it onto a clay slab and repeat the process used to make a base. At this point firm joining can be accomplished by paddling all the seams.

4-16

4-17

4-18

4-19

4-20

4-21

4-22 Chester Old
Cylinder vase
Slab-built stoneware
10 x 3 1/2 inches
Photo: Will Murray

4-23 Caryn Ostrowe
One Hundred Years of Solitude
Slab-built brown and white stoneware
16 x 9 x 8 1/2 inches

4-24

4-25

4-24, To make a bottle from a capped cylinder, one or more spouts are added and a hole for each cut through the top slab. When cutting a hole, slice it in two or more pieces. This allows easy removal of the pieces by shaking them out when the bottle is dry or after the bisque firing.

4-25, Cannisters can easily be built from a capped cylinder by making a cut all the way around near the top. With the cover removed, weld all the interior joints and seal each with a narrow coil. **4-26,** A small slab strip welded to the inside top of the cylinder acts as a flange to hold the cover.

4-26

4-29 Penny Caroline Hood
Covered jar
Slab-built porcelain, salt glaze
8 x 4 1/2 inches

4-27

4-28

4-29

4-30

By cutting a hole in the side and adding feet, a horizontal planter can be made from a capped cylinder.

4-34 Margot Baxter
Slab-built stoneware vase, feathers
7 1/2 x 5 inches
Photo: the author

4-31

4-32

4-33

4-34

Clay can be wrapped around crumpled newspaper. **4-31,** After preparing a slab, place loosely crumpled newspaper in the center, bring one end of the slab over the paper and firmly pinch the slab together all around. Trim the excess clay away. This basic form can be used for many different objects. With the fold at the bottom or side, a spout and pedestal can be added. With the fold at the top, a large hole can be cut in the folded area and a small hole pierced near the top of each side to make a hanging planter.

Changing the length or width of the slab and the size of the paper wad will lead to other interesting shapes. After the piece is completed, allow it to dry slowly. It is unnecessary to remove the paper, because it will burn away in the firing.

43

4-35 Chester Old
Stomach
Slab-built stoneware bottle, ash glaze
12 x 6 x 4 1/2 inches
Photo: Will Murray

4-36 Dennis Parks
Slab-built stoneware urn,
  salt glaze
33 inches high

4-37 Dennis Parks
Slab-built stoneware urn,
  salt glaze
30 inches high

4-36

4-35

4-37

4-38

4-39

4-40

4-41

4-42

4-38, To construct a box form, a rolled out slab is cut into properly measured pieces which are allowed to become firm but not quite leather hard. **4-39,** The side slabs are beveled at 45° on the edges to be joined at the side seams. This increases the joining area and makes invisible corner joints. **4-40,** All the surfaces to be joined are then scored and coated with vinegar. Stand one side piece on top of the base slab and join the two, inside and out, by working clay from one piece to the other with a finger or wooden tool. **4-41,** A small coil of clay is then smoothed into the interior joint as an added seal. The next side is added to the base in the same way and firmly pressed and pinched to the first side. All seams are joined, welded, and coil-filled in this manner until the sides are securely attached to the base and each other. The top joining surface of each side is scored and coated with vinegar along with the facing area of the top slab to be attached. The top is set on the box and secured to the exterior. Liberal use of a paddle is recommended throughout the joining process to insure firm joints and square, sharp corners.

While the box is still sealed, any additional squaring, decorating, or carving should be done. The air trapped inside prevents the box from deforming.

A number of objects can be made using the basic box technique. For example, the closed form may be transformed into a covered container by cutting around the top. **4-42,** For a level cut, draw a guideline by measuring upward from the table at each corner.

4-45 Nancy Peterson
Recipe box
Slab-built stoneware
5 1/2 x 6 x 4 1/2 inches

4-46 Nancy Peterson
Dome container
Slab-built stoneware
8 1/2 x 7 1/2 inches

4-44

4-43

4-45

With the box open, the interior joint of the top is welded and sealed with a coil. **4-43,** A thin slab strip is attached to the inside top of the walls as a flange for a close fit and to prevent the cover from falling off. The cover is then replaced and the box allowed to dry slowly. By drying both top and bottom together, warpage is minimized.

4-46

4-47 Pat Lay
Box
Slab-built earthenware, luster glaze
17 x 17 x 4 inches

4-48 John Costanza
Slab-built stoneware sculpture,
luster glaze
10 x 6 inches

4-50 Christopher Bartlett
Watchtower
Slab-built stoneware
14 x 5 x 2 inches

4-47

4-48

4-49, To make a squared slab bottle, a closed rectangular form is constructed and the spout or spouts are added to the top and welded on. The holes are cut in the top in two or more pieces for easy removal after drying.

4-49

4-50

4-53 Bottle
Japanese Taketori ware
Slab-built stoneware
9 3/8 inches high
Courtesy: The George Walter Vincent
  Smith Art Museum, Springfield, Mass.

4-54 Susanne G. Stephenson
Slab-built stoneware,
  low temperature glaze
10 x 18 x 19 inches

4-51

4-52

4-53

4-54

4-55 Sweet Meat Dish
19th century Japanese Kioto ware
Slab-built stoneware,
    underglaze decoration
Courtesy: The George Walter Vincent
    Smith Art Museum, Springfield, Mass.

4-56 John W. Conrad
Rejoice
Slab-built stoneware, fused stained glass
24 x 16 x 2 1/2 inches

4-57 Sophia Fenton
Wall panel
Slab-built stoneware
21 x 16 inches

4-57

4-55

4-56

4-51, A rectangular slab planter is simply a box without a top. Slab feet, handles, a center-divider, or a rim may be added.

Stiff slab forms need not be rectangular. **4-52,** As an example, by using the same construction methods, a candle lantern can be made with three sides. All stiffened sides to be joined are beveled and, along with the top and bottom, scored, coated with vinegar, and welded together into a closed triangular form. An inch or so from the bottom at the corners, draw a line around for a cupped bottom. Draw a design on each of the sides as well as the top. Plan the design carefully. If the holes are too large, the lighting will be harsh and unappealing. Do all the cutting. After removing the cover, attach a narrow slab around the interior edge of the bottom to act as a flange. Smooth all the cut edges, replace the top, and dry slowly.

Because of its easy construction technique, slab building lends itself to creating large-scale works. As the forms get bigger, technical problems might arise. When building big slab forms, it is advisable to add some sawdust, grass clippings, coffee grounds, or other organic material to the clay before rolling the slabs.

The addition of organic material increases the wet strength of the clay and reduces shrinkage and warping in drying. When the clay is fired, the material burns out leaving an interesting texture and making the finished object lighter in weight. The addition of grog helps in the first and second instances, but it is added weight and has practical limits of addition. Ten to twenty percent is normal. Too much grog makes the clay short and less workable.

An easy way to add the sawdust, if a claymixer is not available, is to slice thin slabs of clay and sprinkle on handfuls of dampened sawdust. Stack the slices together, knead well and repeat the process. For thorough amalgamation, store the clay in closed plastic bags for at least a day—a week is better—before using.

4-58 Marilyn Levine
Jacket #7
Slab-built stoneware
35 x 24 x 5 inches
Photo: Robert Boni

4-58

4-59 Gerald Janosco
End table and footstool
Slab-built stoneware,
   low temperature glaze
Table: 19 x 17 1/2 x 9 1/2 inches
Stool: 14 x 12 1/2 x 9 inches

4-60 Jim Stephenson
Clay block wall
Slab-built stoneware
10 x 7 x 1 feet

4-59

4-60

Some potters have introduced chopped fiberglass into clay for the same reasons. An advantage to using the fine fiberglass strands is that instead of burning out in the fire, they melt to silica and become an integral part of the clay. Noncoated fiberglass cloth can be used to give slabs greater tensile strength while still plastic and when dry. The slabs are made by dipping the cloth into thick slip deflocculated with sodium silicate or Calgon. Without deflocculation, the clay will shrink away from the cloth and crack. The thickness of the slabs can be controlled by the number of cloth layers stacked together. Caution is advised when using this material, however, as some individuals are prone to "fiberglass rot," an extremely uncomfortable rash.

DuPont nylon, 15 denier 120 Bright type, can be added to regular clay in 3/4 inch chopped strands. When thoroughly mixed in, the nylon forms a matrix which makes the soft clay quite durable for constructing paper-thin slab objects. Clay with chopped fiberglass can also be used successfully on the wheel, but clay containing nylon cannot.

The only differences in method when constructing with large slabs instead of small ones are that the large slabs should be somewhat thicker, should be stiffened slowly before using, and require slower drying. Elaborate armatures, complex interior bracing, and super weight are all unnecessary if care is taken at each step. Often, to avoid slumping, it is better to construct a form on its side or longest dimension, dry it, and bisque fire it in this position.

To prevent warping or cracking during drying or firing, a large or complex sculpture form should be put on top of a clay shrinking slab. This slab, made at the same time as the sculpture, dries and shrinks at the same rate and serves to protect the base of the object from distorting.

During construction, liberal use of a paddle is recommended. A slight outward bow to the sides and top will prevent the concave look some slab works have after they have been fired. This occurs because the outside surface and edges of a slab dry faster than the inside, causing uneven shrinkage.

4-61 Barbara Grygutis
Fountain, Union Bank, Tucson, Arizona
Slab-built and thrown stoneware
6 and 4 feet high
Photo: Ray Manley

4-62 Barbara Grygutis
Fireplace
Slab-built stoneware
48 inches high

4-63 Helen Richter Watson
Sculpture
Slab-built and thrown earthenware,
    luster glaze
72 x 25 x 18 inches

4-62

4-63

4-67 Harriet E. Brisson
81 Tiles
Slab-built stoneware, jute, copper pipe
38 x 34 inches
Collection: Leo Marcus

4-64

Trivets, tabletops, wall panels, and murals are also made from slabs. The difference in their construction is only one of scale. To make a trivet, roll out a slab at least 1/2 inch thick and stamp, carve or cut the design. **4-65,** When stiffened to almost leather hard, turn over the piece and carve a waffle pattern. This results in more even drying of the piece and reduces warping. It also diffuses the heat when the finished trivet is in use. For minimum warping, cover the top and bottom of the trivet with sheets of newspaper and place it between plaster boards to dry.

4-65

4-66

4-67

4-68 Author
The Garden
Slab-built earthenware, wood
14 x 34 inches
Collection: Mr. and Mrs. Joseph Epstein

4-69 Tom Supensky
Odalisque by the Numbers [After Ingres]
Slab-built earthenware,
  luster glaze, decals
18 x 10 x 9 inches

4-70 Author
Candelabra
Slab-built stoneware, wood
54 x 22 inches
Collection: Mr. and Mrs. Milton Smith

4-68

4-69

4-70

Tabletops and low-relief panels are made in the same way as a trivet. When making these items it is advisable to work from a drawing that takes into account the shrinkage of the clay when fired. If the clay shrinks 15 percent, the drawing should be 15 percent greater than the final table or frame.

After rolling a large slab of proper thickness, the drawing is placed directly on the clay and traced with a dull pointed stick or pencil. Only after all the incising, adding of clay, texturing and correcting have been completed should the clay be cut into pieces of manageable size. It is visually more effective if cuts can be made along lines of the composition rather than the standard horizontal-vertical grid slices. When the clay has stiffened to not quite leather hard. turn over the pieces and waffle cut them. If some parts of the relief are higher than the others, it is important that they be hollowed to the same thickness as the rest of the work to avoid splitting or explosion in the kiln.

To firmly attach the glaze fired pieces, the tabletop or panel must be clean, uncoated, and have a slightly roughened surface. It is not necessary to use cement beds or grout to adhere the tiles. Best results have been obtained using 3M brand CTA-11 tile setting mastic. TEC brand 21F mastic is also acceptable. Follow directions on the label. Many other brands of ceramic tile mastic will not accept the weight of handmade tiles, so test sampling is recommended. GE Silicone Sealer also works well when joining clay to wood or other materials.

55

4-71

Clay is most effective in architectural murals when used in high relief. The procedure is much the same as in making smaller wall panels. If depth is anticipated in the mural, slab sections of 2 or 3 inches thick should be rolled out. In this case a departure from the usual pizza method of making slabs is advisable. Slamming fistfuls of clay down on a canvas-covered floor will prevent air pockets. Heavy paddling before rolling will also help. After rolling, the surface is modeled to completion. Sections not being worked should be kept covered with plastic. Occasional misting with water will keep the clay workable until the entire piece is completely modeled. When the work is done and the clay stiffened to almost leather hard, the mural should be cut into convenient pieces. The pieces are then hollowed to a thickness of about 3/8 inch throughout to facilitate drying. Leave a rim on the underside of each piece at least 1-inch wide to provide sufficient bearing surface for tile mastic to adhere to when mounted on wood panels.

If the fired mural is to be a permanent installation, the cavity of each piece is filled to level with neat cement or dryset mortar. This gives a greater bearing surface to each piece before being set into a fresh mortar bed which has been laid up on the wall.

4-72

CHAPTER 5 Throwing

The magic of the potter's wheel has often been the motivation that brings many people to ceramics, only to discover that throwing can be just plain hard work. The techniques described in this chapter have been used successfully by the author in his own work and to teach others of all ages and backgrounds. Some similarities to other methods may be noted, since there is no one correct way. Of course, the best way to learn to throw is to sit at a wheel and do it.

The First Steps

It is essential that well kneaded clay of the proper consistency be used for throwing. After kneading, good studio practice calls for cutting and making clay balls which are then weighed. In this way it will soon be learned how much clay is needed to make an object of a certain finished size.

To start, three-pound balls of clay are recommended. With this easy-to-handle amount, most people can throw a cylinder 4 inches wide and 8 inches high with little difficulty.

The basic wheel types will be discussed in the chapter on Kilns, Wheels, and Studio Equipment. What is most important is that the wheel be smooth running and comfortable to the user. A sitting position is recommended, although some potters prefer to stand.

A few basic hand tools, either purchased or homemade, are needed. An elephant ear sponge or other thin, natural sponge is important for applying or removing water, a pin tool or hatpin aids in trimming uneven tops of pots, a wooden knife is used to trim excess clay from the base of the pot, and a twisted wire or nylon fishline is needed to cut the pot from the wheelhead. A container of very thin slurry placed near the wheel is necessary to provide a lubricant. Clay absorbs clear water and rapidly softens.

Sit close to and comfortably over the wheel, with all tools, water, and clay within reach. Drop a ball of clay on the center of the wheelhead while the wheel is either still or slowly turning. Try not to mash the ball out of shape when doing this. Great controversy exists over which direction the wheel should turn. Generally, right-handed people turn the wheel counterclockwise and left-handed people will be most comfortable with the wheel turning clockwise. If the wheel is turning counterclockwise, the right hand will be the top hand and the left, the side hand. Clockwise, the reverse is true. Once this has been determined, do not vary positions.

5-1

The following method works well for both small and large amounts of clay, with no changes in positions needed. The side hand elbow should rest against the hipbone allowing the back to lend needed pressure. The top hand arm should be locked firmly against the side of the body, allowing the shoulder to apply pressure. In this way the body does the work and the arms and wrists will not tire so easily.

5-2

5-3

5-4

Centering

Centering the clay on the wheel is the important first step in making any pot. If not done successfully, it will hamper all the other steps necessary to bring a pot to completion.

Lubricate the clay and hands with a thin film of slurry. Too much water will make the clay too soft to handle. Bring the wheel to top speed when centering. The faster the wheel is turning, the less time and pressure are required to move the clay.

5-3, With the side hand resting against the side of the clay, slowly increasing downward pressure should be applied just behind the center of the ball with the top hand palm securing the clay firmly to the wheelhead. Pressure should then be gradually increased with the palm of the side hand used to center the clay. Quick motions with either hand or undue changes of pressure will force the clay off center. Lubricate the clay sparingly as needed by applying slurry on the ball with the sponge.

Forming a Cone

After the clay has been put relatively on center, the top hand is brought down the side directly opposite the side hand. **5-4,** Both palms then slowly squeeze the clay upward into a narrow cone. Two or three passes should accomplish this. It is important to use slowly diminishing even pressure, or the top of the cone might be torn off. The top hand palm then pushes the cone down while light pressure is applied by the side hand to guide downward movement. **5-5,** With the side hand braced, the clay can move nowhere else but on center.

Repeating this important process three or four times helps center the clay inside the ball as well as outside, making it more elastic and workable.

The next step is to open a hole in the center of the ball. The simplest method is to place both palms opposite each other on the sides of the spinning ball with the thumb tips touching the center, and the arms still braced against the body. Arch the thumbs and push them downward into the clay until they are about three-quarters of an inch from the bottom. **5-6,** Do not raise the wrists or in any way alter the position of the hands, for this upsets control of pressure. Instead, if the thumbs do not reach all the way down, push the walls of clay downward with the web between thumb and index finger of both hands. Increasing pressure by the palms will prevent the ball from going off center. **5-7,** When the correct depth is reached, push both thumb tips toward the palms to widen the hole. **5-8,** Then cup the palms slightly under the ball to collect the clay at the base.

The foregoing procedure must be carried out each time a pot is to be made. If any part of it is incorrectly or poorly done, the pot will not succeed.

An alternate method of opening the hole can be used by those who have difficulty coordinating their thumbs or when working with very large amounts of clay. Instead of placing the thumbs over the center of the ball, all the fingers of the top hand are positioned together over the spinning ball of clay with the thumb resting on the side hand for leverage. **5-9,** The fingers are then pushed into the clay to the proper depth and squeezed toward the side hand to widen the hole.

It should be noted that long fingernails will hamper any work in throwing clay and should be trimmed as short as possible.

58

5-5

5-6

5-7

5-8

5-9

5-10

59

Making a Cylinder

After opening the hole, the position of the hands and arms are changed. The arms should now be braced against the sides of the body. **5-11,** With both palms facing and fingers pointing straight down, the side hand goes inside the hole and the top hand directly opposite on the outside with both thumbs interlocked. It is essential that the hands be held in this manner, otherwise the motion of the wheel will be counter to the direction of the hands and the fingers will dig in and cut the clay rather than allow it to slip through.

Starting at the bottom of the hole, cup the fingers slightly and increase the pressure of the fingertips in a pincers fashion. With the wheel turning rapidly, begin to draw the hands upward, pulling the clay. The outside hand must move up a bit first to get directly opposite the inside hand: otherwise the clay will tend to move out instead of up. Slowly reduce the pressure near the top, leaving a slightly thicker rim. **5-12,** Too much pressure might tear off the upper portion and destroy the cylinder. Apply light, even lubrication only when required.

Repeat these hand movements. Start at the bottom each time and slowly decrease the pressure between the fingertips as the top is neared. **5-13,** At the top, slight downward pressure with the thumb or index finger will keep the lip level. As the cylinder grows taller the wheel should be allowed to slow down proportionately. If the wheel remains at too high a speed, centrifugal force will carry the top off center and the piece will invariably collapse. If the cylinder walls are uneven or large spirals appear in the walls, the ratio of wheel speed and upward hand motion must be corrected. The slower the wheel turns, the slower the hands should rise. In order to keep the hands perpendicular to the wheel while pulling up the clay, the forearms remain braced against the sides, while the elbows slowly slide to the rear. This action prevents the hands from moving in an arc.

The pin tool can be used to correct an uneven lip. Locking the arms against the side of the body for stability, grasp the pin with the outside hand, leaving enough pin to pass through the cylinder wall. **5-14,** Slowly ease the pin through the moderately spinning cylinder until the point touches the waiting inside hand, then quickly lift up. **5-15,** This leaves a smooth, level lip which can then be thickened and rounded with a sponge or piece of leather. A thick rim looks better than a knife edge, holds glaze better and helps prevent the cylinder from warping.

5-11

5-12

5-13

5-14

5-15

Removing a Cylinder

Cutting a piece from the wheel is a simple three-step process. First, hold the wooden knife in the outside hand like a pencil. **5-16,** With support from the other hand, make an angled cut into the base of the moderately turning cylinder to remove excess clay. **5-17,** Next, make a flat cut underneath the excess to free it from the wheelhead. Then take the excess from the wheel. **5-18,** Finally, to cut the finished cylinder free, grasp the cutting wire firmly in both hands and draw it taut beneath the slowly turning cylinder, across the wheelhead toward the body. **5-19,** Remove the piece from the stopped wheel by opening wide the index and second fingers of both hands and lifting lightly under the cut base, giving the wheel a slight turn to break the friction.

The preceding processes should be repeated continually until a natural rhythm is developed between wheel, clay, and potter. Because the cylinder is the basis for all other forms made on the wheel, it is extremely important to master its formation before attempting to go on to other shapes.

A good test of skill is to raise a 3-pound ball of clay into a 4-inch diameter, 8-inch high, even-walled cylinder in three pulls. If it takes more pulling or if the cylinder is not the proper size, it is an indication that the technique has yet to be mastered.

One way to check on the shape of a pot while it is in progress is to set up a mirror on the opposite side of the wheel. With this, a full view of the work may be seen without having to let go or change position.

5-18

5-16

5-17

5-19

5-20

Trimming

After the cylinder has been removed from the wheel, it should dry slowly until it is stiff enough to be turned upside down for trimming.

5-20, A wide variety of trimming tools are commercially available in many different styles. It is also possible to make trimming tools using spring steel, bandsaw blades, and the like. In either case it is important that the cutting edge be kept sharp and the loop stiff to prevent "chatter" marks when trimming. If these marks should appear on a pot, they can be easily removed by trimming the pot as the wheel is turned in the opposite direction. The tool should, of course, be sharpened before being used again. Round wire modeling tools are generally not successful when used for trimming.

Before putting a pot on the wheel to trim, feel the wall thicknesses to gauge the amount of work needed. To center a pot for trimming, invert it on a slightly wet, slowly turning wheel and tap it into center.

5-21, A more accurate and safer way to secure the pot to the wheel is to invert it on the slowly turning dry wheel and hold a finger near the side of the pot. If the finger touches in only one place, stop the wheel and move the pot a short distance directly away from where the finger touched. Continue to do this until the pot is centered. Secure the pot with three equally spaced clay lumps, being careful not to damage the rim. When first learning to trim, use a pin tool to mark the exact location of the footring on the bottom of the pot. A ring that is too narrow will cause the pot to wobble, while a ring that is too wide will make the pot look bottom-heavy.

5-21

5-22

5-23

Secure the outside hand arm against the side of the body or leg and hold the trimming tool with the cutting edge at a 45° angle to the clay surface. Place the inside hand arm against the leg or side and rest the thumb of that hand against the other hand for support. The middle finger should also rest lightly on the center of the pot to help prevent the pot from accidentally flying off the wheel. **5-23,** Bring the wheel up to throwing speed and gently begin to cut away the excess clay. If properly done, long strips of clay should literally fly off the pot. If the tool gets stuck in the clay, remove the pot and allow it to stiffen some more. If short, grainy pieces of clay come off, the pot is too stiff to trim well and should be disposed of. It is sometimes possible, however, to soften the clay by scoring concentric rings into the pot with the pin tool and wetting the area with a sponge before proceeding.

Normally a footring the thickness of the pot wall and no deeper than 1/4 to 1/2 inch is all that is necessary.

After the foot has been trimmed, it should be smoothed with a wooden tool or piece of leather. Trimming marks are very obvious in heavily grogged clay. **5-24,** Rethrowing over the marks with a wooden tool will push the grog back into the clay and make the marks less noticeable.

5-24

When footing a bottle or other narrow-necked form, which might fall over when it is inverted, a trimming chuck should be used for better stability. The chuck can be a flowerpot, jar, or hand-thrown and bisque-fired cylinder made especially for this purpose. Center the chuck on the wheel and secure it with three equally spaced lumps of clay. The clay sticks better if the bisque chuck is first soaked in water. Invert the bottle into the chuck, center, secure it, and trim. **5-25,** An inexpensive carpenter's level can be helpful with centering.

Chucks can also be used when trimming pots with rims too wide to rest on the wheel head. Center and secure the chuck and invert the pot onto it.

"Wet" chucks can also be helpful when trimming. Center some clay on the wheel and throw a thick-walled cylinder.

Open it to the width necessary to safely support the bottle to be trimmed. **5-26,** Cover the rim of the cylinder with a piece of cloth, secure the bottle in the chuck and trim. **5-27,** A solid mound of clay can be centered and shaped to the inside curve of a large bowl and used as a chuck.

Some potters prefer not to foot at all but simply throw a thinner base and smooth the bottom, to save time. However, a foot serves many purposes, not the least of which is an aesthetic one. A good foot elevates the pot making it seem fuller and more rounded. It also provides a good place to end the glaze, allowing the clay color to show and preventing a runny glaze from sticking the pot to a kiln shelf. A foot also provides a smaller, more even surface to rest on a kiln shelf. A flat bottom might catch on the shelf and warp the pot.

5-25

5-26

5-27

5-28 Laurie Adams
Thrown porcelain vase
9 inches high
Photo: Bill Byers

5-29 John T. Forgey
Drum
Thrown stoneware, animal skin
17 x 9 inches

5-30 Daisy Brand
Thrown stoneware urn
19 x 14 inches

5-28

5-29

5-30

5-31

5-32

5-33

5-34

5-35

Pedestals—Feet

Instead of trimming deep into a thick base, a taller foot or pedestal can be made separately and attached. Allow it first to stiffen, invert it, and trim it. Then trim the bottom of the pot without a foot. Score the surfaces of pot and foot where they are to be joined and coat with vinegar. Place the foot on top of the inverted pot and check for center. **5-31,** Check the foot for level before sealing the parts together. Add coils to insure a firm joint.

Another way to make a pedestal foot is to throw it directly on top of a trimmed pot. Do not remove the pot from the wheel after it has been trimmed without a foot. Score the bottom and coat it with vinegar. **5-33,** Secure a doughnut of soft clay to it. With a light touch, center the doughnut and throw a cylinder with an outward flare at the top. Keep enough extra clay at the lip to make a broad rim for the pot to stand on.

Slowly dry the piece upside down, then fire upright.

5-36

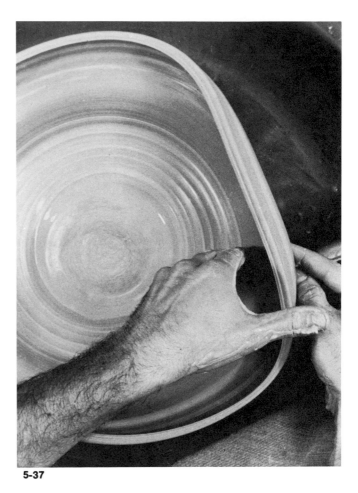

5-37

Making a Bowl Form

The next logical step after learning to throw a straight-walled cylinder is to make a bowl form. All of the procedures necessary to make a cylinder must first be carefully carried out: properly kneaded clay, centering, opening a hole, and pulling up the wall. Assuming a 3-pound ball of clay is used, the wall is made thicker and shorter than the usual finished cylinder. With the wheel turning at moderate speed, place one finger of the ouside hand lightly against the side of the rim. **5-36,** Starting at the bottom with the inside hand, slowly raise the fingers upward while gently pushing out. After two or three light passes, a thin walled bowl is complete. Finish the rim with a damp sponge or piece of leather, cut away the excess clay from the foot, and gently remove the bowl from the wheel.

This technique is known as the *stretching method*, for in actuality that is what is being done to the clay walls. The inside hand is stretching the clay outward from the center while the outside finger prevents the wall from going out of round. Care must be taken not to stretch the clay too thinly because stretch marks will appear and, if the wall is taken out too far, it will split open. If marks begin to appear, it is an indication that the walls are becoming too thin. This may be remedied by using the outside hand to push inward while the inside hand steadies the lip.

Ribs made of metal, wood, or rubber can be used to aid in stretching large pieces. Overuse of these tools can render the finished work slick and lifeless.

68

5-39 Steve Haworth
Thrown stoneware bowl
18 inch diameter

5-40 Jim Cantrell
Thrown and cut stoneware bowl
5 x 15 inches

5-39

5-38

5-40

If larger or wider bowls are to be made, a round bat, which is a clay form support, should be used. Bats can be made of wood, fiberboard, linoleum, or other stiff material, but, generally, plaster bats are best. To secure a bat to the wheel, spread a small amount of thin slurry over the wheelhead and on the underside of the bat. Press the bat onto the wheel with a twisting motion until it no longer moves. If the bat does not adhere in a few seconds, scrape off the slurry and start again or use another bat.

Large bowls are made in the same way as small ones, except that wheel speed becomes a very important factor. The wider the bowl, the slower the wheel should turn. **5-37,** Centrifugal force from a rapidly spinning wheel might cause the bowl to open too fast and collapse.

Another way to make a wide bowl utilizes a smooth stick. After a wide low cylinder is thrown, the inside hand holds the end of the stick near the bottom of the cylinder, while the outside hand slowly lowers the stick onto the rim of the moderately spinning cylinder. **5-38,** Pressure is continued until the desired curve of the wall is attained. Then the bowl is finished as usual. Carefully remove the bat by sliding a spatula or long knife under it to break the suction.

When making bowls, or any other pots for that matter, experiment with the shape of the rim. Often a simple form can be made much more expressive or elegant by the way in which the rim is finished.

69

5-41

5-42

5-43

Plates

A plate or platter is just a very wide, low cylinder, but a somewhat different technique is employed to insure against splitting. **5-41,** After securing a bat to the wheelhead, center a well-kneaded ball of clay in the usual manner, but continue to press the ball down and outward until it is almost the desired diameter. **5-42,** Then, using the braced inside hand, begin to open a hole in the center by moving the hand partway to the outside. Change the direction of the inside hand and push down and back into the center. This action of throwing toward the center compacts the strained clay and helps prevent the plate from "S-crack" splitting while it dries. Continue to open outward and push back until the bottom of the plate reaches the final diameter. Make all the necessary changes to finish the bottom before pulling up the wall. **5-43,** Raise the wall, make a rim, and finish the lip in the usual way. **5-44,** The rim can also be made by opening it with a stick. By using these methods, the common accident of collapse by overextending the plate rim is prevented. Cut the excess clay away from the base with a wooden knife. Remove the bat from the wheel without releasing the plate. Later when the plate has stiffened, it can simply be lifted from the bat with no cutting wire needed. In this way, thinner, flatter bottoms can be made which later require only a minimum of trimming. **5-45,** On very wide platters a double foot rim can help prevent slumping when the piece is fired. Dry the finished plate slowly, upside down on a thin bed of fine grog to prevent warping.

5-46 Robert Parrott
Thrown and cut stoneware plate
22 inch diameter

5-47 Nancy Peterson
Mirror
Thrown stoneware, coil decoration
12 inch diameter

5-44

5-45

5-46

5-47

Throwing off the Hump

5-48

Many production potters use a technique of throwing which enables them to make numerous pieces at one sitting without having to knead separate balls of clay. This method is known as *throwing off the hump*, or *lump*. It is also very useful for making small pots, covers, or spouts.

After kneading a large ball of clay, center it on the wheel and pat it into a cone shape. Draw the desired amount of clay to the top and center it, using the normal method. Throw the object as usual. Trim excess clay from its base, making a deep notch below the bottom of the pot. Slow the wheel down, pass a cutting wire through the notch to release the pot, and remove it. Recenter the top of the hump and continue throwing.

5-49

5-50

Bottles

Bottles also begin as cylinders. **5-51,** A straight bottle form can be made by pulling the upper portion of a cylinder a bit taller with a thinner wall. **5-52,** With both hands directly opposite each other on the otuside, use the tips of thumbs and index fingers to slowly squeeze in and upward on the moderately spinning cylinder. Repeat this action, called *collaring* or *necking*, keeping thumbs and fingertips equally spaced to avoid twisting the clay. Each time a pass is made, the clay wall becomes thicker. **5-53,** After two or three squeezes put a finger inside and outside the neck and pull up the clay wall. Continue collaring until the neck is well formed. Then finish the lip, cut excess clay from the bottom and remove as usual.

To make a rounded bottle, after the cylinder is thrown, only partially neck the top. **5-55,** Then insert a sponge-on-a-stick or a throwing stick into the bottle and stretch the lower portion of the form to the desired curve. The neck is then finished in the usual manner and the bottle is cut from the wheel.

For added fullness in a bottle form, stop the wheel just before finishing the lip and gently blow into the bottle. If the walls are evenly thin, the entire form will expand and round out.

5-51

5-52

5-53

5-54

5-57 Bette Casteel
Blue Plum Bottle
Thrown stoneware, reduction ash glaze
6 1/2 x 3 inches

5-58 Roberta Griffith
Bottle
Thrown porcelain, luster glaze
9 1/2 x 6 inches

5-59 David Atkinson
Thrown and assembled stoneware bottles
14 x 8 x 7 inches

5-55

5-56

5-57

5-58

5-59

Pitchers

For best results in making a pitcher, it is first necessary to throw a thin-walled cylinder. **5-60,** Stretch some fullness to the form and collar it near the top. **5-61,** To make the spout, pinch in the lip using the tips of the thumb and index finger. **5-62,** Then, while the thumb and finger are still in position, draw the inside of the lip over the outside with a moistened finger of the other hand. This allows the pitcher to pour without dripping. Cut excess clay from the base and set the pitcher aside to stiffen.

In order to make a handle, first shape a small piece of clay into a cone. **5-63,** Holding the clay in one hand, wet the other and grasp the clay, drawing downward while evenly reducing pressure. Repeat this procedure until the clay has been pulled longer than the desired length. Wet the hand only when necessary to prevent the clay from becoming too soft. If splits appear in the handle, break off the clay at this point and continue to pull if there is enough clay. Otherwise, start again with more clay. To give the handle more grace after

5-60

5-61

5-62

5-63

5-64

5-65

making the clay long enough, position the thumb in front of the clay and curve the index finger behind. **5-64,** Then apply light pressure while drawing the hand downward to create a groove and alter the profile of the handle from round to wide and thin. **5-65,** Next, take the bottom end of the clay and swiftly bend the handle to connect the end to the lump. Set this down on the lump and allow it to stiffen while trimming the pitcher.

When the pitcher and handle are ready to join, cut the handle from its lump, score the ends and matching points on the pitcher, soften these with vinegar, and then press the handle firmly to the pitcher. **5-66,** Seal all joints carefully, adding a tiny coil if needed to smooth the handle into the form. Allow the finished pitcher to dry slowly under plastic. Because the handle tends to dry faster than the body of the pitcher, the handle may be wrapped with a strip of damp cloth to help equalize drying. A better way to slow the drying would be to coat the entire handle and joined areas with wax resist. The wax later burns away in the bisque fire.

5-66

5-67 Robert Parrott
Pint, quart and two-quart pitchers
Thrown stoneware

5-68 Adele Firshein
Thrown stoneware pitcher
8 x 6 1/2 inches

5-69 Georgette Zirbes
Thrown stoneware pitcher and mugs
Pitcher: 9 inches high

5-67

5-68

5-69

Covered Containers

Think of a covered container as a bowl with a plate on top and it becomes simple to make. The important factor to keep in mind is that somehow the plate, or cover, must be made to fit well. There are many different configurations that the lips of the bowl and cover could take, but basically they fit into three categories. The first is a smooth-lipped bowl with the retainer flange as part of the cover, the second with the flange as part of the bowl and the third a "rose petal jar" type with a domed cover that fits over the bowl's upturned lip. To be sure that the cover fits well, a measuring stick or pair of calipers is useful. It is important that the bowl and cover be made during the same session; otherwise the shrinkage might be different and prevent a good fit.

To make the first type of container, with the flange in the cover, throw a bowl with a smooth rim. **5-70,** Accurately measure the inside diameter of the rim and set the bowl aside. Throw a shallow bowl about the same diameter as the first, leaving a little extra clay at the rim. **5-71,** Slowly widen this bowl until the caliper tips measure into the middle of the rim. Lightly push down the clay on the outer portion of the measurement until a flange of about 1/4 inch stands upright. **5-72,** Using a wooden tool or fingernail make sure that the flange is properly square before finishing the outer edge of the lip. Always check the measurements before cutting the cover off the wheel. It is better to have the flange a hair wider than the given measurement to insure a snug fit later. A measurement that is too narrow causes sloppy, loose fitting covers. The variation in shrinkage is caused by differences in the orientation of clay particles in the horizontally thrown cover and vertically thrown bowl.

When the parts are leather hard, trim the bowl as usual and then trim the cover without a foot. While the cover is still secured to the wheel, weld a small doughnut of very soft clay onto the center of the dome. **5-73,** With a very light touch, throw an open knob. Knobs or handles can also be hand fashioned, if desired, but must not be made too thick or closed because they will explode in firing. After trimming, place the cover on the bowl and set both aside to dry slowly. Drying and firing the pieces together helps prevent undue warping.

5-70

5-71

5-72

5-73

5-74

5-75 Jim Cantrell
Thrown stoneware storage jar
11 1/2 x 11 inches
Photo: Neal Cornett

5-76 John Perri
Thrown stoneware covered jar, ash glaze
16 x 12 inches

5-75

5-76

5-80 Jim Cantrell
Thrown stoneware covered jar
16 x 6 inches

5-77

5-78

5-79

The second type of bowl and cover combination has the flange inside the bowl. To do this, a bowl is thrown the normal way but extra clay is left at the rim. **5-77,** Once this has been done, gently push the inner half of the rim downward at least 3/8 to 1/2 inch. Try to make the flange level and squared out from the wall. A square cut wooden tool helps. **5-78,** Finish the edge of the flange and lip. Take a measurement of the inside diameter of the lip before removing the bowl from the wheel. The cover is a shallow bowl with its outside diameter slightly larger than the caliper measurement to allow for shrinkage. When leather hard, the cover is trimmed and a knob added as before. Trim the bowl and allow both parts to dry together.

5-80

5-85 Rochester Folk Art Guild
Covered jar
Thrown and incised porcelain
9 x 8 1/2 inches

5-81

5-82

5-83

5-84

5-85

The third kind of container is often used for storage because, if properly made, it provides a better seal at the cover than the others. To achieve this end, the bowl is thrown taller than the desired height. **5-81,** The lip is slowly coaxed inward toward the center by moving the outside hand over the inside hand, which remains stationary. **5-82,** Move the outside hand back and reverse the procedure, holding the outside hand still and raising the inside hand to stand the lip upright. **5-83,** Use a wooden tool to square the exterior of the flange. Take the measurement of the outside diameter of the flange and throw a dome-like cover whose inside diameter equals the measurement. After trimming, dry and fire the pieces together. A more traditional version of the rose petal jar has a third part, a lid which fits on the lip inside the cover. This added piece is thrown as a small bowl the diameter of the inside of the jar rim, with an outward turned lip extending just to the outer edge of that rim.

5-86

5-87

5-88

Teapots

The true test of skill regarding ability to throw well on the wheel is the execution of a teapot. The challenge is to make it well balanced, easy to handle, with a spout that pours without dripping and a cover that fits snugly. If each of the objects previously discussed has been successfully mastered, a good teapot can be made with little difficulty.

Teapots are generally made in four parts: body, cover, spout, and handle. The first three parts should be thrown and properly measured at the same sitting, then allowed to stiffen equally. **5-86,** The body of the teapot should be made thin-walled, full, and with a small opening at the top. **5-87,** The cover should be made upside down with a long flange to prevent it from falling out during pouring. **5-88,** Make the spout like a bottleneck with a flaired rim and sharp edge to pour without dripping.

5-89, When the parts are ready to trim, pull a handle large enough to grip with the whole hand and graceful enough to complement the shape of the body.

Trim the body and the cover so that they fit together. Then throw a knob on the cover using a small doughnut of soft clay. **5-90,** If an exhaust hole is desired, it might be best drilled in the center of the knob instead of elsewhere on the cover where it might detract from the design.

5-89

5-90

Line up the spout so that it is at a good pouring angle and not too low on the body. **5-91,** The tip of the spout must rise above the maximum liquid level; otherwise the tea will run out. **5-92,** After the spout alignment has been marked on the body, drill a number of small holes with a potter's knife or drill bit inside the mark. These aid in the smooth flow of liquid and keep tea leaves from pouring out. **5-93,** Score the surfaces to be joined, apply vinegar, and weld the spout to the body. **5-94,** Align the handle directly opposite the spout, mark the spots where it is to be joined, score the surfaces, apply vinegar, and weld the handle firmly to the body. **5-95,** Replace the cover and allow everything to dry slowly. Wax resist can be used on the handle, knob, and spout tip to retard drying.

5-91

5-92

5-93

5-94

5-95

5-96 William A. Coombs
Thrown stoneware teapot
11 x 8 inches

5-97 Adele Firshein
Thrown stoneware teapot
8 1/2 x 6 1/2 inches

5-98 Gilbert Bassin
Thrown stoneware sculpture
19 x 10 inches

5-96

5-97

5-98

Large Sculptural Forms

Large sculptural forms can be constructed using wheel thrown parts. It is often best to have a sketch with dimensions of the object to be built. After planning the sizes and joining of the pieces, all the parts should be thrown, trimmed and allowed to stiffen before being assembled. The assembly process is the same as before, scoring the surfaces to be joined, applying vinegar, and then welding the parts together, adding tiny coils if needed. It is very important that a sufficient number of holes are drilled in all strategic points to allow steam to escape during the firing. The form must be completely hollow with no enclosed spaces or solid parts. A well-executed figure with a blown-off arm could result if a hole is inadvertently left out.

5-99 Victor Spinski
Machine Form
Thrown and molded earthenware,
  luster glaze, decals
5 1/2 feet high

5-100 Turker Ozdogan
Gordian Knot
Thrown hollow ring stoneware form
92 x 22 inches

5-101 Donna G. Burgess
Medieval Chess Set
Thrown stoneware and porcelain, wood
4 inches high

5-99

Dry Throwing

Dry throwing is an advanced technique that can be used to successfully throw very large, thin-walled pots without the usual problems of wobbling and collapse. The major advantage of this method is that because no water is used in throwing, the pot does not get soft and slump. In fact, during the throwing process, the clay actually becomes stiffer, allowing more time to refine the form.

For best results the clay must be well homogenized and stiffer than usual. At first, amounts of 5 to 10 pounds should be used until the process becomes familiar. Amounts of 25 to 50 pounds or more can be easily thrown after sufficient practice.

Centering is carried out using normal wet methods. After the hole has been opened, completely dry the hands. From this point on slurry is not used. The hands must be held in the vertical pincers position, directly opposite each other. Only the tips of the fingers should touch the clay wall. Most difficulties with this method occur because the fingers are not properly positioned.

5-100

5-101

5-102 Gary T. Smith
Thrown stoneware sculpture
28 x 18 inches

5-103 Carolyn Long
Bride
Thrown stoneware
14 x 6 inches
Photo: Robert Pack

Because the clay is stiff, the wheel can be turned faster for throwing, but to prevent twists, pulling up must be done more slowly.

Bring the cylinder up to an even thickness on the first few pulls. Then draw up the top third much thinner than the rest. Pull the middle third next and then the bottom portion. Between each of these pulls, make a full length draw to keep the cylinder centered. After pulling the clay to its full height, the stretching method can be used, dry, to complete the form. Either the fingers or throwing ribs can be used, provided they are kept dry.

To make a narrow neck, throw the top section in and upward, using one hand inside and the other outside. The usual necking method does not work well in this case. A dampened sponge to smooth the lip is all the water necessary to finish the piece. Remove the pot from the wheel in the regular way.

Because the clay is stiff to begin with and tends to set up faster than usual when drying, care should be taken that it is dried evenly.

5-102

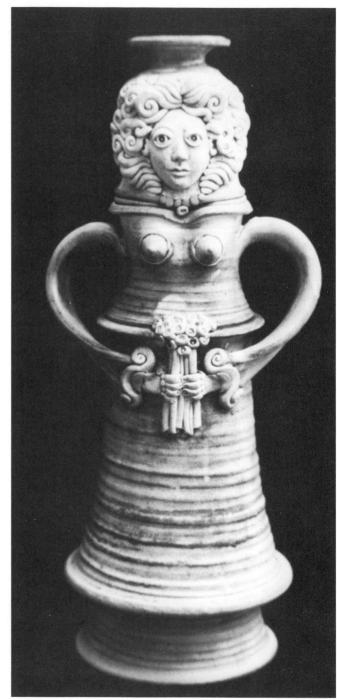

5-103

CHAPTER 6 Design in Clay

6-1 Jim Cantrell
Teapot
Thrown stoneware
6 inches high

6-2 Irvin Tepper
Airplane Crash Teapot
Handbuilt porcelain, china paint
12 x 14 inches

When first working in clay, the main concern is just to make an object hold together. Once this has been accomplished, the imagination is freed to explore the development of a good design.

Good design is a combination of vision and common sense. It is akin to the difference between looking and seeing. Looking both ways before crossing a street involves merely a quick glance to insure survival. Seeing an object involves a conscious effort to focus not only the eyes but the mind as well; to actively discern the object's parts; to compare its shape with objects of a similar nature; and to decide its individual merits. While the public cannot see an object until it is a *fait accompli,* for the artist, a work must be visible in the mind's eye before it is ever constructed.

While technical facility is an important part in the execution of a ceramic form, no amount of expertise can substitute for the lack of a well conceived design.

The following principles of design apply universally without regard to time, place or media. They will serve as an invaluable guide to developing well designed ceramic objects.

A purpose should be evident in the work. For example, a utilitarian object should, by its design, fulfill its intended function in the best possible way. This does not mean that it must follow traditionally assigned silhouettes. Some designs have remained relatively unchanged over time because they are pleasing and serviceable. Others have not changed due to force of habit or lack of imagination. In either case, designs should be looked at critically, with a constant eye toward improvement. Just because teapots have for centuries had one handle and a pouring spout, it is not necessary to stay rigidly within that format. A teapot may not require a typical handle if there is another way to lift it.

6-3 Jim Cantrell
Pitcher
Thrown stoneware
10 inches high

6-4 Thom Collins
Sculpture
Thrown stoneware
19 x 20 inches

6-5 Edward Camp
Free Form No. 3
Thrown porcelain, lacquer
29 x 11 x 9 inches

6-3

6-4

The parts of an object should reflect their importance. A small-bodied pitcher with a large spout might make a better watering can. If the main function of a pitcher is to hold liquid, then the body should obviously be larger than the spout. The spout need only be sufficient to direct the flow of liquid. The handle should be large enough to hold comfortably for lifting, transporting, and pouring.

Balance is an important consideration. In most clay ware, symmetry is automatically imposed because the object must balance to stand upright. Symmetry is not necessary as long as the central axis of a form falls within the circumference of its base. A piece should also have a visual axis around which all the parts eventually converge in a manner that can stimulate and please the viewer. Odd numbers of appendages, spouts, feet or handles can offer a dynamic balance that even numbers do not.

6-5

6-6 Mary Lou Alberetti
Raku sculpture
15 x 20 x 15 inches

6-7 Edward Camp
Construction No. 1
Thrown stoneware, flock, overglaze,
  luster glaze
16 x 7 x 7 inches

The form of the object should be developed in harmony with the materials used. Work done in clay can exploit its flexible plastic quality, emphasize volume or bulk or utilize texture to enhance the surface.

6-6

Contrast creates impact. A simple cylindrical form, for example, can provide a ground over which a complex surface treatment can easily move. A subdued surface on a multispouted organic form directs the interest to its convolutions of volume. In either case, if form and surface are both boldly executed, confusion will dominate, and the total object will be less effective. Contrasting color is also a way to draw attention to the significant part or parts of a form. The plain colored interior of a pot offers good contrast to a more actively colored exterior. To achieve dynamic contrast between positive and negative space, one should be greater than the other. For example, a bowl which is wider than it is deep has more visual appeal than another with equal dimensions.

6-7

6-8 Gordon Orear
Sculpture
Thrown stoneware, brass
14 1/2 x 13 1/2 inches

6-9 Author
Fountain
Slab-built and thrown stoneware
40 x 17 x 17 inches

6-10 Randy Miseph
Sculpture
Thrown stoneware, flock, luster glaze
7 x 3 x 15 inches

6-8

6-9

Simplicity can make the most elegant statement. A work which expresses a well conceived idea can motivate the viewer to thoughts and emotions even beyond those intended by the artist. This does not mean that for an object to be effective it must be plain. Even a sprawling, multiunit form can have simplicity if there are no extraneous parts to detract from the whole.

6-10

Tactile quality is part of the experience of a work. People like to touch ceramic objects. Drinking or eating from smooth ceramic sufaces makes either activity more pleasurable. Sculptural forms which play rough areas against smooth, capture light, and offer both a visual and a physical tactile sensation.

Boldness and exaggeration give life to an object. Weak curves, lazy linear changes from belly to shoulder of a vase, a thin or nonexistant lip, all contribute to a lackluster form. A high bulging shoulder which sweeps inward to a narrowed neck finishing in a well articulated lip can elevate a vase and make it seem larger and fuller.

6-11

6-11 Sophia Fenton
Sea Urchin
Slab and coilbuilt stoneware
15 x 13 inches

6-12 Author
Bottle
Thrown stoneware
11 inches high

6-13 Helen Richter Watson
Sculpture No. 3
Slab-built and thrown stoneware,
  luster glaze
68 inches high

6-12

6-13

93

6-14

6-15

6-16

Proportion can create strength and excitement in a form. It can also kill it. A tall narrow vase appears to continue its upward movement while a short, squat form seems heavy and dull. For a start, a ratio of 3:1 can be applied to the proportions of an object. A piece will often have more interest if its height is three or more times its width. The same is true of an open form which has its width three or more times its height. This is not intended to be a hard and fast rule, but more often than not, a relationship such as this does help create a more impressive form. The volume proportion of an object can exert control over its visual weight. Using the same ratio of thirds, a form with its greatest width at the top will have a *dynamic* or light appearance. A similar form with its widest part in the lower third will appear *static* or heavy. One with the widest part in the middle will be *neutral*.

6-17

6-18

6-19

Each object has its own optimal weight. For instance, if a cup feels heavier than it ought to, its aesthetic appeal is immediately diminished. Using thin slabs and coils or throwing thin walls will usually give the most satisfactory results. It is probably not possible to make a clay object too light.

Proficient execution is necessary to carry an idea to successful resolution. If the work is sloppily joined, poorly thrown, or carelessly glazed, the best ideas and intentions are lost.

All of the foregoing considerations must be present to some degree just to make an object serve its intended function! Something more is needed to elevate a form beyond the prosaic. Call it style, grace, or beauty, it is this quality that separates the artist from the artisan, the aesthetic from the merely efficient.

95

6-20 Formula Vee Racing Car
Builder: Zeitler
Owner: Robert Francisco
Photo: the author

6-21 Terminal Building
Dulles International Airport
Architect: Eero Saarinen
Photo: the author

6-22 City Hall, Toronto, Canada
Architect: Viljo Revell
Photo: the author

6-20

6-21

Some people feel that a person is born with artistic sensitivity. Others feel that this sensitivity can be learned. In all probability, each person has an innate artistic understanding which needs only to be brought out and honed to a fine edge. Formal study can hasten this process and offer a wide range of exposure to ideas and influences. Individuals can gain insight on their own as well as in school. To be creative requires action. Inspiration does not strike like lightning; it develops. Imagination can be stimulated by historical and contemporary ceramic works. Direct copying, however is plagiarism and makes no useful contribution. Examine man-made designs in other disciplines and media—fashion, automotive, architecture, painting, film. Look at designs in nature—growth forms, crystalline structures, geometric progressions. Develop a sense of curiosity; find out what makes things work. Make sketches of ideas and keep notes.

Be dissatisfied with the end product. Try to improve on a form and continue to develop it toward a better solution. A masterpiece is not made, but it may grow with time. Even then it is great only to those who see greatness in it.

Movement in ideas and forms should continue. Making a "hot item" and reproducing it endlessly can bring about stagnation. The clayworker stops developing, the form ceases to grow, and the viewer/buyer appreciation does not advance. Situations change, needs change, conditions of life change; and the clayworker should be attuned to these changes.

6-22

l

l Author
Life Forms
Slab-built stoneware, glaze, slip-
    fused stained glass
4 x 18 feet
Courtesy: Rochester Institute
    of Technology
Photo: Edvard Deering

II. G. Portanier
Platter
Thrown earthenware, oxide decoration
18 inch diameter

III. Charles Malin
Soft Chevroned Mollusca
Slab-built earthenware,
    terra sigillata decoration
30 x 16 x 6 inches

IV Author
Vase
Thrown porcelain, local reduction
8 inches high

V John Heller
Soup tureen
Thrown and handbuilt porcelain,
    luster glaze
6 x 10 inches

II

III

IV

V

VI Bill Stewart
All American Hawkman
Handbuilt earthenware, luster glaze
18 inches high

VII William Suworoff
Raku vase
13 x 16 inches

VIII Susanne G. Stephenson
Box
Slab-built porcelain, reduction, low
    temperature and luster glazes
14 1/2 x 10 x 17 inches

VII

VI

IX William Wilhelmi
Lotus Jar
Thrown and pierced earthenware,
    unglazed underglaze13 x 5 inches

X Patti Warashina
Hillside Kiln
Handbuilt earthenware,
    low temperature glaze
23 x 23 x 20 inches

VIII

IX

X

XII

XIII

XIV

XV Georgette Zirbes
Spiritual Connection
Stoneware and fiber, luster glaze
81 inches high

XVI

XVII

XVIII

XVI Robert M. Winokur
Covered jar
Thrown stoneware, ash glaze
20 inches high

XVII Elsa Rady
Bottle
Thrown porcelain, copper reduction glaze
7 1/2 x 6 1/2 inches

XVIII Jim Hurt
Covered jar
Thrown stoneware, ash glaze
14 inches high

XIX

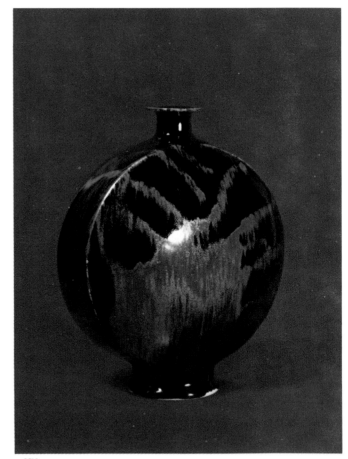

XIX Brother Thomas
Vase
Thrown porcelain, Chun-type
   reduction glaze
13 x 15 inches
Collection: Dr. Edward Brewer
Photo: Bullaty-Lomeo

XX Brother Thomas
Vase
Thrown porcelain, Honan-type
   reduction glaze
9 x 7 inches
Collection: Mr. and Mrs. Frederick Bloom
Photo: Bullaty-Lomeo

XX

6-23 Vase
19th century Japanese Satsumi ware
Thrown stoneware, underglaze,
    overglaze, slip decoration
14 1/2 x 12 inches
Courtesy: The George Walter Vincent
    Smith Art Museum, Springfield, Mass.

6-24 Richard Shaw
Couch and Sinking Ship
Handbuilt earthenware, acrylic paint
15 x 14 x 36 inches
Courtesy: Quay Gallery

In the evolution of a form there is first the recognition of that form as an object of some use. As the understanding of the object increases it is taken into its second stage, becoming highly refined to gain its ultimate utility. The third stage brings the object beyond utility into the realm of the symbolic. For instance, the Paleolithic hand axe was a crude, hand-held stone implement for pounding. As the ages progressed the axe was made of metal, refined and shaped until it could cut in a single stroke. The final step occurred when the axe became a ritual implement made of jade or jewel-encrusted gold, which stood as an emblem of power.

The same is true today of clay. The crude concave mud form which held liquid came to a high state of refinement in Chinese and Japanese ceramics which have been emulated for centuries. In recent times a number of clayworkers have taken the third step and elevated their work beyond utility, into the symbolic.

What of these nonutilitarian objects? What kind of criteria are necessary to understand them? The new wave of ceramics appears, at first, to throw aside function and negate all the principles of design. Victor Papanek states in his book, *Design for the Real World*, that, "the cancerous growth of the creative individual expressing himself egocentrically at the expense of the spectator and/or consumer has spread from the arts [and] overrun most of the crafts. . . No longer does the artist, craftsman, or in some cases the designer, operate with the good of the consumer in mind; rather, many creative statements have become highly individualistic, autotherapeutic little comments by the artist to himself."

This is too often, but not always, the case. If the concept of a work is carefully thought out, if its story, political or satirical social comment are well expressed, then the design elements will usually fall into place. The color, size variation, shape, and position of its parts may not be as important as the strength of the statement. Upon closer examination, many examples of this direction in claywork do adhere relatively closely to the basic principles of design—balance, contrast, boldness, simplicity and proportion, with the overriding principle being its purpose, that of stimulating the viewer's emotions and thoughts. However, if the execution of the object does not evidence technical proficiency, it will fail to rise above the autotherapeutic stage.

6-23

6-24

97

CHAPTER 7 Traditional Decorating Techniques

7-1 Vase
Chinese, K'ang-hsi Period (1662-1722)
Thrown porcelain, polychrome overglaze
18 1/2 x 8 5/16 inches
Courtesy: Worcester Art Museum

7-1

Most people cannot resist the urge to decorate a plain surface, whether it be a stretched canvas, a subway wall, or a clay pot. All too often they succeed only in diminishing the value of the original object. This is particularly true of ceramics. For centuries the potter's work was regarded as just a form upon which the renderings of an accomplished decorator were to be placed. Although this holds true even today in some commercial operations, most potters now make and decorate their own work. Unfortunately, many of them overdo it. If decoration is thought of as an integral part of a design, the results will be much more effective.

Each of the techniques described earlier has its own set of intrinsic decorations: pinch marks, coil lines, texture from the rolling surface, or throwing ridges. Often these are interesting enough in themselves to make a pot exciting to look at and hold. Additional methods of decorating can be introduced at different stages and conditions of the clay. Some decorations can be applied when the clay is still plastic, others when the clay has stiffened to the leather hard state or when dry and still others after the bisque fire.

Although most of the examples shown here have been executed on wheel-thrown pieces, there is no reason why they cannot be effectively adapted to other shapes.

Plastic

While the clay is still plastic, it may be *pressed* or *pinched* with the fingers to create a relief decoration. When doing this, support the wall of the pot from inside to prevent deforming. On a thrown piece, it is best to press or pinch while the pot is still on the wheel so that the rim can be recentered after the clay has been worked. **7-2, 7-3**

Stamping a repeat decoration on a pot can be done with many found objects: for instance, a stone, seashell, or piece of wood. Support the wall while pressing a dry stamp against the pot. A stamp, made by modeling a piece of clay with a small stump attached to the back, should be dried and

7-4 Author
Hanging planter
Thrown stoneware, pinched decoration
7 x 11 inches

7-2

7-3

7-4

7-5

7-6

7-7

7-6 Vase
Egyptian, ca. 2nd century B.C.
Earthenware, stamped decoration
3 inches high
Courtesy: Museum of Fine Arts, Boston
   Egyptian Expedition Fund

7-7 Steve Haworth
Plate
Thrown stoneware, stamped decoration
15 inch diameter

7-9 Katalin Radnoti
Thrown stoneware, stamped decoration,
low temperature glaze
22 1/2 x 13 1/2 inches

7-8

7-9

7-13 Bowl
Mexican, ca. 750-900
Earthenware, modeled decoration
6 1/2 inches high
Courtesy: Museum of the
American Indian, Heye Foundation
Gift of Harmon W. Hendricks

7-10

7-11 Leon F. Moburg
Bottle
Thrown stoneware, scratched decoration
8 x 6 inches

bisque fired. Plaster poured into a small paper cup can be carved into sharply defined decorations after it has hardened. In each case, a design that is undercut will pull on the clay and not print well. **7-5, 7-8**

Decorative textures can be *scratched* into the surface of a pot with a toothed scraper, sawblade, twig, comb, or any other similar object. **7-10**

Small coils, cut bits, patches, or a thick paste of clay can be *modeled-on* or *appliquéd* directly to the plastic wall of a pot while still soft. Harder clay pieces must be applied using vinegar. **7-12**

Following the bisque fire, a glaze which thins out, or breaks, over protruding parts should be used to achieve the maximum effect of the relief surfaces thus created.

7-11

7-12

7-13

7-14 Elsa Rady
Dish
Thrown porcelain, incised decoration
11 inch diameter

7-15 Rochester Folk Art Guild
Vase
Thrown porcelain, carved decoration
6 x 5 inches

7-16 Rochester Folk Art Guild
Vase
Thrown stoneware, carved decoration,
    salt glaze
16 x 7 1/4 inches

7-14

7-15

Leather Hard

When the clay has reached the leather hard state, trimming tools, dentist tools, or other sharp instruments can be used to *incise.* or carve in, decorative motifs. These same tools can be used to *pierce,* or cut through, the clay form. **7-17, 7-18**

Excising is done by carving away the background around a decoration, leaving the image in a raised relief. Use a thicker-walled pot for this method to allow sufficient depth for the carving. **7-21**

7-16

7-17

7-18

7-19 Incense Burners
19th century Japanese Arita ware
Cast porcelain, pierced decoration
left: 10 1/2 x 5 inches;
right: 6 1/2 x 4 1/2 inches
Courtesy: The George Walter Vincent
    Smith Art Museum, Springfield, Mass.

7-20 Rochester Folk Art Guild
Candlehouse
Thrown stoneware, pierced decoration
9 1/2 x 7 1/2 inches

7-22 Vase
14th century Mayan
Earthenware, excised decoration
8 x 7 1/2 inches
Courtesy: Museum of the
    American Indian, Heye Foundation
Gift of Harmon W. Hendricks

7-19

7-20

7-21

7-22

7-24 Rochester Folk Art Guild
Platter
Thrown porcelain,
  brushed slip decoration
14 inch diameter

7-25 Rochester Folk Art Guild
Platter
Thrown porcelain,
  brushed slip decoration
16 inch diameter

Decorating with colored *washes, slips,* or *engobes* is carried out essentially in the same way, although the three materials differ somewhat from each other. A *wash* is nothing more than a coloring oxide, such as copper carbonate, iron oxide, or cobalt oxide, mixed with water. Very little colorant is needed to give a strong tint. A *slip* is a clay slurry to which colorant has been added. *Engobes* are glaze materials combined to make colored clay-like slurries. **7-23**

All of these materials can be brushed, poured, dipped, or sprayed on a pot in thin coats to provide decorative color in contrast to the clay body. Slips of different colors are sometimes built up in layers, resulting in a low relief decoration known as *pâte-sur-pâte.* **7-26**

After a thin coat of slip has been applied to a pot, a *sgraffito* design can be scratched through it with a pin tool to bring out the clay color. **7-29**

7-23

7-24

7-25

7-26

7-27 Jim Hurt
Vase
Slab-built stoneware,
    brushed slip decoration
12 x 5 x 5 1/2 inches

7-28 Bottles
19th Century Japanese Agano ware
Thrown stoneware,
    stippled engobe decoration
11 1/2 inches high
Courtesy: The George Walter Vincent
    Smith Art Museum, Springfield, Mass.

7-30 J. David Broudo
Thrown stoneware vase
Sgraffito with oxide wash decoration
17 x 8 inches

7-27

7-28

7-29

7-30

7-31

7-32 Covered Jars
18th and 19th century Japanese
Thrown stoneware, mishima decoration
left: 21 1/2 inches high;
right: 3 inches high
Courtesy: The George Walter Vincent
    Smith Art Museum, Springfield, Mass.

7-32

A *mishima*, or inlayed, decoration can be made by first carving a design into a pot. The carving is then filled with thick colored slip. After the slip has set up, the excess is scraped away, leaving a smooth, flush surface. This works best when the clay and slip have the same shrinkage factor. Ideally, the colored slip should be made from the clay body being used.

105

Slip trailing can best be accomplished using a plastic squeeze bottle or a syringe. In earlier times, a goose quill on the end of a small bisque fired bottle did the job well. Depending upon the viscosity of the slip, the decoration will either run, lie flat, or make a thick relief. Mix the color into the slip and strain it through a 60-mesh sieve to remove any lumps. Make a few practice trailings to check the consistency of the slip before using it on the actual piece. Keep the trailer close to the surface and squeeze the tube with steady pressure. **7-33**

Trailed slips can be *combed* or *feathered*. Pour an even coat of slip over a freshly made platter. Trail a simple design immediately, using one or more colored slips. Then draw a comb with few teeth or a feather tip lightly through the slip to create zigzag effects. Tap the platter lightly to settle the slips.

7-33

7-34

7-35 Ilse Johnson
Thrown stoneware platter
Slip trailed decoration
22 inch diameter

7-35

7-34 Water Jar
18th century Japanese Kyushu ware
Thrown stoneware, slip trailed decoration
13 3/4 x 15 inches
Courtesy: The George Walter Vincent
    Smith Art Museum, Springfield, Mass.

7-36

7-37

106

7-37 Plate
16th century Japanese Hizen ware
Thrown stoneware, combed decoration
13 inch diameter
Courtesy: Museum of Fine Arts, Boston
  Morse Collection

7-38 Leon F. Moburg
Covered jar
Thrown stoneware, sliptrailed
  and feathered decoration
13 x 5 inches

7-40 Tripod Vase and Cover
Wedgewood Jasper ware, 1786
Blue and white cast porcelain
7 7/8 x 5 1/2 inches
Courtesy: Wadsworth Atheneum, Hartford
Photo: E. Irving Blomstrann

7-38

7-40

Sprigs are low relief clay decorations made from shallow press molds with no undercuts. After a sprig stiffens and shrinks it can be dropped out of the mold and firmly joined to the pot with vinegar.

7-39

Dry

Clay can also be decorated after it has dried. *Engobes* or *oxide washes* can be applied to the surface by brushing. They can be poured, sprayed, or dipped as well, but must be thinned beforehand to prevent undue buildup. **7-41**

Wax resist can be used to brush a decoration on before applying an engobe or oxide wash over it. The wax prevents the engobe or wash from adhering to the decorated area.

A *stencil* made of Japanese rice paper or paper towel can be placed against the clay before brushing or spraying on an engobe. **7-43**

Commercially prepared *underglazes* or *underglaze pencil* can be used to draw decorations on dry clay. **7-44**

7-41

7-42

7-43

7-44

7-45 John Goodheart
A Potter's Odyssey
Slab-built earthenware,
  luster glaze, underglaze pencil
20 x 14 x 6 inches

7-46 William Wilhelmi
Phoenix Unfrequent
Covered cakeplate
Thrown earthenware, underglaze pencil,
  metal finial
14 x 12 inches

7-45

7-46

109

7-48 Plate
18th century Chinese
Cast porcelain, underglaze decoration
9 5/8 inch diameter
Courtesy: Worcester Art Museum
  John Chandler Bancroft Collection

7-47

7-48

Bisque

Some of the decorating techniques just mentioned can also be used on bisque fired ware. Applying *engobes* and *oxide washes* to a bisque fired piece allows the color to be absorbed into the glaze instead of the clay, which occurs when applied to dry work. **7-47**

After applying *engobes* or *oxide washes*, *sgraffito* through them to the bisqued clay for more delicate lines than when the technique is used on leather hard clay. **7-49**

Wax resist can be used to brush on a decoration before the work is glazed. Because wax prevents glaze from adhering to the bisque, the clay provides a color and texture contrast to the glazed surface after the firing. **7-51**

Underglazes can also be applied to bisque fired ware. **7-52**

7-49

7-50 Rochester Folk Art Guild
Thrown stoneware mugs
Sgraffito through oxide decoration
4 1/2 x 3 inches

7-53 Irvin Tepper
Lemon Meringue Sea
Slab-built earthenware, underglaze
22 x 16 x 11 inches

7-50

7-51

7-52

7-53

Glaze Application

Improperly applied glaze can detract from the appearance of an otherwise well formed ceramic object.

Before glazing, the piece should be clean and free of dust and hand oils. With the eyes shielded, blow off any dust. Wiping will force the dust into the clay pores. Oily pieces should be washed with soap, rinsed, and thoroughly dried before glazing.

If it seems necessary, a quick swipe on the bisque with a damp sponge just before glazing will reduce glaze absorption and prevent an application that is too thick. This can be better controlled, however, by adjusting the viscosity of the glaze before use.

Wax will prevent glaze from being absorbed into the bisque and should be applied to the foot or anyplace else that glaze is not wanted, such as lips and rims of covered containers. If wax drips onto parts of a piece that are to be glazed, scrape and then sand it off; otherwise the glaze will not adhere. Unwanted wax can also be melted off with a lighted match, or the entire piece can be put into a kiln and heated to 200°C (392°F), which will volatilize all the wax. Reapply the wax when the piece has completely cooled.

Pour

The interior of nearly all pots can be glazed by pouring. After properly mixing and sieving a glaze, it is poured into a pot to about half full. **7-54,** The pot is revolved three or four times while being tipped slowly over a bowl, allowing the glaze to run out. If excess glaze runs down the outside of a piece, allow it to dry and then brush it off with a toothbrush or other stiff brush. Wiping with a wet sponge will only force the glaze into the clay pores.

If a pot, such as a lantern, has holes cut through it, cover them with masking tape before pouring glaze inside. After the glaze has dried, remove the tape. In the case of a teapot, cover the spout opening with a neatly trimmed piece of masking tape before pouring the inside. Leave the tape on until after the outside has also been glazed, preventing the outside glaze from running into the interior. When the glaze has dried, remove the tape and touch up the lip with a small brush.

After the inside has been glazed, the work should be allowed to dry thoroughly before attempting to glaze the exterior. Glaze powders adhere to the pot because the water is drawn into the bisque wall. If more glaze is applied to the outside soon after the inside has been glazed, the clay will not absorb the proper amount of water and the coating will be too thin. Forced drying often has the opposite effect. A pot warmed under a heat lamp or in a kiln absorbs too much water and causes a thick glaze coat.

7-54

7-55

The quickest way to coat the outside of most ceramic objects is by pouring. **7-55,** Invert the piece onto a funnel, jar or similar support placed in a bowl on a bench wheel. Two sticks, metal rods, or a grate can be used to support large objects over a bowl.

7-56, Fill a pitcher with glaze and then pour the glaze over the piece while turning the wheel around three or four times. A large syringe filled with glaze can also be used for pouring. Wait until the shine disappears, then remove the pot and let it dry completely.

When pouring glaze on a piece with a handle, such as a cup or pitcher, glaze the handle first and then rotate the pot while pouring to give it an even coating.

After the pot has completely dried, clean the foot well by scraping off excess glaze with a knife or cleanup tool. Then remove all traces of glaze with a wet sponge.

Removing glaze from the foot and bottom of a pot is known as *dry footing,* which must be done if pots are to be fired directly on the kiln shelf. Aside from eliminating the need for stilts or pins (which have a nasty habit of breaking) to support the pot during firing, dry footing also has an aesthetic function. It shows the fired clay color in contrast to the glaze.

When inside and outside glazes are different, it is often more pleasing to have the inside glaze on the rim as contrast to the outside color. To do this, carefully scrape all the glaze from the rim when dry and reapply two or three coats of the interior glaze with a small brush. An alternate method of doing this is to brush wax over the inside glaze on the rim before pouring the outside color. This prevents the outside glaze from adhering to the glazed rim. After pouring, simply wipe the excess glaze off the wax with a damp sponge.

Lumps of glaze on the rim, caused by pouring, should be carefully smoothed away with a fingertip after the glaze has dried to prevent running in the fire.

If cracks or pinholes appear in the glaze after it has dried, it is an indication that the glaze coating may be too thick. Try smoothing over and filling in the holes by gently rubbing the glaze with a circular motion of the fingertips. Chipped off pieces may be filled in by gently dabbing on fresh glaze with a finger or small brush. If there are too many cracks, drips, holes, or an uneven surface, it is best to scrape off the glaze, wash the piece, thoroughly dry it, and start again.

Several glazes can be poured on the outside of a pot if they are applied immediately, one after another. However if the piece is allowed to dry before another glaze is applied, the first glaze will be pulled off because of the rapid re-wetting. A syringe or spoon can be used to selectively pour glazes over small areas.

7-56

7-57

7-59 J. David Broudo
Thrown and paddled stoneware bottles
Oxide decoration, dipped in ash glaze
6 to 18 inches high

Dip

Small objects can be quickly glazed by dipping. Hold the pot by the foot or bottom and dip it at an angle into a bucket of glaze. Turn the piece back and forth two or three times to cover it evenly with glaze and then remove it. Another way to dip a slightly larger piece is to fill the inside to the top with glaze and hold for about five seconds. Then turn the pot over and immediately plunge it into the glaze for about five more seconds. Remove the pot from the glaze and continually turn it to prevent glaze from accumulating on one part of the lip while it dries. A pot can be dipped into more than one glaze for added interest.

Another method of dipping, requiring somewhat more dexterity, can also be employed, but a little practice is needed to master it. The pot is first pressed upside down into the glaze, then swiftly jerked upward—but not out of the glaze. It is then plunged back down and shaken slightly. The upward jerk creates a partial vacuum which is filled by glaze on the downward motion.

Attempting to glaze large pieces with this method often requires the preparation of too much glaze to make it worthwhile.

7-59

7-58

Brush

Brushing on a glaze is not as easy to do properly as it might appear. Too many people attack a pot with a brush as if painting the side of a barn. First, good quality brushes should always be used. Japanese hare's fur or goat hair brushes are recommended for their ability to hold large amounts of glaze. If these are not available, other high quality, soft, long natural bristle brushes can be used. To allow two or three even applications to be brushed on, the glaze should be thinned.

Charge the brush well by dipping the bristles fully into the glaze with a stirring motion. This will also prevent the glaze from settling in its container.

When applying the glaze, do not hold the brush perpendicular to the object. It should be held at a slight tangent, lightly touching the surface to allow the bisque wall to draw the glaze off the brush. **7-60,** Because glaze comes off the brush heaviest at the start of the stroke and lighter at the end, each stroke in one direction should be immediately covered starting from the other end. Brushing should continue at a steady pace until the entire piece is covered. If too much time elapses between coatings, later brushstrokes will pull off earlier applications.

7-60

7-61

115

Spray

Spraying is the technique which can be used to give the most even glaze coating. Occasional hand spraying can be done in a well-ventilated area; but if spray glazing is done regularly, proper equipment is essential. A spray booth with a good exhaust fan and ventilator filter system, a quality air compressor capable of at least 25 psi (pounds per square inch) and a medium duty spray gun are needed for safety. It is also a good idea to wear a face mask when spraying to prevent inhalation of the dry powders.

Place the object to be glazed on a bench wheel in the booth. Mix the glaze through at least a 60-mesh sieve to the smooth consistency of light cream. Fill the spray gun and hold it approximately eighteen inches from the object. Spray with a slow vertical sweeping movement while slowly revolving the bench wheel. If the gun is too close to the work or is not moved enough, the glaze will pile up and run. **7-62,** Keep the gun and object moving to prevent glaze from building up a shiny wet surface. Spray from above and below the object to insure an even glaze coating. **7-63,** Continue to spray until a fuzzy surface is built up. Then allow the glaze to dry before cleaning the foot well with a damp sponge.

If the inside and outside glazes are different, protect the previously glazed interior by inverting the pot or by covering the opening with a jar cap, paper or masking tape.

Unlike other glazing techniques, the sprayed glaze surface is quite powdery and therefore should be handled as little as possible to prevent smudging.

Major drawbacks to this technique are the wasted glaze sprayed into the booth and the amount of time consumed. The former can be scraped up periodically, a sample test fired, and possibly reused. The time lost can never be reclaimed.

7-62

7-63

7-64

7-65

7-66

Other Decorating Techniques

7-64, After glaze has been applied to a pot, a *sgraffito* decoration can be scratched through to the bisque which will leave delicate lines in the fired glaze.

Applying glaze over glaze is known as *onglaze* decoration. Majolica and Faïence ware are early examples of this method. The technique gives best results when the base glaze has been sprayed on and the onglazes applied with light brushstrokes.

7-65, *Oxide washes* can also be applied on top of a glaze for striking decorative effects.

7-66, *Glaze/wax/glaze* is a decorating method achieved by immediately brushing a wax resist decoration onto a freshly glazed pot and then applying a different color glaze over it.

117

7-67 Vase
12th century Chinese Tz'u-Chou ware
Thrown earthenware,
  sgraffito through glaze
18 3/4 x 13 3/8 inches
Courtesy: Worcester Art Museum
  Gift of Alfred K. Pearson

7-68 Scalloped Plate
16th century Italian
Earthenware, majolica decoration
11 inch diameter
Courtesy: Worcester Art Museum

7-69 Niderviller, ca. 1775
Plate with Plums
Earthenware, faïence decoration
10 inch diameter
Courtesy: Wadsworth Atheneum, Hartford
Photo: E. Irving Blomstrann

7-67

Colored clays offer effective results when used as the means of decoration for a ceramic object. Additions of 1 to 15 percent of a coloring oxide or commercial body stain will give a pronounced color to a clay. Although earthenware and stoneware clays can be used, white-firing clays give the brightest colors. The colorant may be added by weight to a dry clay mix but kneading it into damp clay is quicker. Test samples of varied percentage additions should be made and fired, both glazed and unglazed, before large amounts are mixed.

7-68

7-69

7-70 Gerry Williams
Bottle
Thrown porcelain,
  brushed slips over glaze
10 x 4 1/2 inches
Photo: Bill Finney

7-71 Cow Creamer
Bennington Pottery 1850-60
Scroddled Ware colored clay decoration
6 1/2 x 5 inches
Courtesy: Wadsworth Atheneum, Hartford
Photo: E. Irving Blomstrann

7-72 Elizabeth C. Kron
Sculpture
Slab and coil built
  colored earthenware clays
10 x 10 x 3 1/2 inches
Collection: the author

7-70

7-71

The colored clays can then be kneaded into or pressed onto pinch forms, coil and slab-built objects or wheel-thrown pots. Care should be taken to prevent the clay colors from muddying each other on the exterior of the object. If this does happen, a light sandpapering after the ware has dried should restore color definition.

7-73 Linda Arndt
Dish
Slab-built colored porcelain
24 x 24 x 4 inches

7-72

7-73

7-74 Patrick Siler
Box
Slab-built colored clay
8 x 8 x 8 inches

7-75 Rochester Folk Art Guild
Vase
Thrown colored porcelain
11 x 6 1/2 inches

7-76 Amphora
Greek, ca. 6th century B.C.
Earthenware, black figure decoration
24 1/2 x 14 5/8 inches
Courtesy: Worcester Art Museum
  Austin and Sarah Garver Fund

Terra sigillata, although actually denoting early Roman stamped ware, has come to refer to early Greek and Roman earthenware decorated with a shiny dark surface. The coating is not a glaze but a refined clay slip. Terra sigillata is usually prepared from a low temperature red clay as follows: Mix a thin slip of 20 percent clay and 80 percent water (distilled, if possible). About 1/10th of 1 percent of a deflocculant can be added to keep the clay particles in suspension. Ball milling will help make a homogeneous slip but is not necessary if the slip is thoroughly mixed. Allow the slip to settle in a container for at least a day. Drain off the standing water. Then take out the top third of the clay slip for use and discard the remainder. If desired, the slip may be diluted and mixed again. After it has settled, another usable portion can be drawn off and its remainder discarded.

Terra sigillata should be applied very thinly on damp or dry ware. A heavy coating could crack during drying and shrinking. To achieve a harder, glossier finish, the terra sigillata coated surface may be burnished before firing with the back of a spoon or other smooth instrument. Firing terra sigillata at cone 06 (991°C/1816°F) or lower brings out the color and shiny surface. At higher temperatures the surface tends to dull. Most terra sigillata fires from red to ochre to brown in oxidation and to black in reduction. If colors other than the natural tones are desired, a batch of 30 percent dry terra sigillata, 70 percent water with 3 percent colorant added can be used. Cobalt, copper, chrome, manganese, and stains will give interesting colors. Although a well fired terra sigillata may give the appearance of a glaze, it does not make the ware water proof.

7-74

7-77 Charles Malin
Succulently Plaid
Slab-built earthenware,
  terra sigillata decoration
30 x 16 x 6 inches

7-75

7-76

7-77

120

CHAPTER 8 Adapting Commercial Decorating Techniques

Over the past few years, contemporary clayworkers have begun to draw upon certain commercial processes to broaden the possibilities for embellishing the surfaces of their work. These decorations are applied after the ware has been finished and glaze fired. For sharp bright effects, the ware should be fired with a hard gloss glaze. It is possible to use matt glazes with these technquies, but results may vary because of the inherently rougher surface.

Before applying decoration with any of these techniques, the ware should be cleaned with denatured alcohol and thoroughly dried.

Overglaze

In earlier times, decorators ground their own combination of overglaze pigments and fluxes in a medium of various oils and turpentine. Today, many companies have developed a large array of ready mixed colors which can be applied directly from the jar. It is important to note which type of medium, such as mineral spirits or lavender oil, is used in a particular overglaze. Thinning with the wrong medium can spoil the decoration.

Overglazes should be applied with good quality camel hair brushes for lining and banding. Large areas can best be covered by using an airbrush, a refined version of the glaze spray gun. The usual glaze gun has too coarse a spray for successful overglazing.

Because overglazes are usually made of finely ground prefired ingredients, a thin coating is all that is required to afford good color. Mistakes should be wiped off immediately with a piece of cloth or cotton swab dipped in mineral spirits or the manufacturer's recommended thinner. The overglaze should be thoroughly dried before firing.

It is important that overglazes be fired to the exact temperature recommended by the manufacturer. Many of the colors have extremely short firing ranges and overfiring by as little as 10 or 15 degrees could cause the color to disappear. Because a good oxidizing atmosphere is required, an electric kiln should be used. Overglazes fire in the range of cone 019 to 014 (668°-834°C, 1234°-1533°F.) Glass glazes, which react like overglazes, can be fired on glass as well as on fired glaze in the cone 022 to cone 020 (585°-625°C, 1085°-1157°F) range. Fired overglaze flaws can be removed by using a china paint eraser.

8-1 Vase
19th century Japanese Satsumi ware
Thrown stoneware, overglaze decoration
14 1/2 x 12 inches
Courtest: The George Walter Vincent
 Smith Art Museum, Springfield, Mass.

8-3 John Goodheart
Night Rainbow
Thrown earthenware,
  impressed, sprigged, engobe
  decoration, luster glaze
24 inch diameter

8-2

8-3

Luster Glaze

The earliest known examples of luster glazing are those from the Mediterranean area dating from the early ninth century. These bowls and plates were first glaze fired then decorated with thinned glazes charged with salts of metals, such as copper, and fired again.

Although it is possible to prepare luster glazes in the studio, the procedures are long, costly, and relatively dangerous. Many of the chemicals are toxic and hazardous to the eyes. Fortunately, a number of companies market a large selection of ready-to-use metallic and pearlescent lusters along with liquid bright metals, such as gold and palladium.

Because lusters are in suspension and are not dissolved mixtures, the containers should not be shaken. Material which collects at the bottom should be discarded. If it is necessary to thin a luster glaze, use only the medium recommended by the manufacturer.

Lusters can be poured, brushed, or airbrushed in a thin coat over a fired glaze and should then be dried thoroughly before firing. It is best to use a separate brush for each color because luster is difficult to remove completely from the bristles. Brushes should be cleaned with denatured alcohol after each use.

An oxidation firing should proceed slowly to about 450°C (842°F) with the kiln door open to allow the escape of fumes from the organic medium. The kiln is then closed and fired to the recommended temperature. To insure good oxidation, the spy holes may be kept open for the duration of the firing. Most luster glazes mature in the firing range of cone 020 to cone 018 (625°-696°C, 1157°-1285°F). Overfired lusters burn out.

Luster glazes can be given great depth and brilliance by repeated reglazing and firing. Interesting effects can be obtained by mixing different luster glazes together, applying them and firing. Firing a transparent color luster glaze over a fired metallic luster can also bring about striking results.

To remove unwanted fired luster glaze, use a china paint or gold eraser. If the glaze should tarnish, it may be cleaned and buffed with a silver dusting cloth. Anything more abrasive could scratch the glaze off.

8-4 Pitcher
Staffordshire ware, ca. 1810
Cast porcelain, luster glaze
6 1/2 inches high
Courtesy: Museum of Fine Arts, Boston
    Gift of Theodora Lyman

8-5 Patti Warashina
Airstream Turkey
Handbuilt earthenware, luster glaze
20 x 10 x 6 inches

8-6 Randy Miseph
Platter
Thrown stoneware, luster glaze
17 inch diameter

8-4

8-6

8-5

8-7

Decals

Used commercially since the 1800s, onglaze lithographs, or decals, are traditionally made by printing ceramic glazes on thin paper coated with gelatin or starch. The surface of the ware to be decorated is then coated with varnish or decal size. While the varnish is still tacky, the print is placed face down on the ware and rubbed with a dampened stiff brush until completely secured. After the varnish has dried, the heavy paper backing the decal is washed off. The ware is thoroughly dried for at least eight hours at room temperature and then fired.

The advent of *watermount* decals has made the entire process of application much easier. In this process, the image is lithographed right side up on simplex paper coated with a soluble material. A thin coating of lacquer is applied over the print. To apply the decal, cut it out of its mounting sheet and place it in a pan of room temperature water. Sufficient time should be allowed only for the paper to become completely soaked. Prolonged soaking can spoil the adhesive quality of the lacquer. **8-8,** The decal is drained and then slid face up from its backing onto the clean ware and adjusted into position. **8-9,** Using a stiff piece of cardboard or a rubber squeegee, force all water and air

8-8

8-7 Plate
Stevenson and Williams Company,
   ca. 1820
Cast earthenware,
   transfer printed decoration
10 inch diameter
Courtesy: Worcester Art Museum
   Bequest of Grenville Norcross

8-9

8-10

8-10 Author
Bicentennial Commemorative
Stoneware, decals, luster glaze
12 inch diameter
Collection: Mr. and Mrs. Zalman Davlin

8-11 Howard Kottler
Look Alike Plate
Cast porcelain, decals, luster glaze
10 inch diameter

8-12 Donald P. Taylor
Technicolor Grant
Thrown stoneware, artist's own decals
6 1/2, 8, 10 inch diameters

bubbles from the center outward. Failure to do this will result in poor resolution when the decal is fired. Surplus water and residue must be removed from the ware with a dry cloth.

Complicated forms can be decorated by first warming the ware and then molding on the decal with the fingers. The decal will stretch slightly to fit. Any wrinkles can easily be squeegeed out. Interesting and humorous effects can be developed by selectively combining portions of various decals.

Decals can be made in the studio by using normal silkscreen methods to print oil-based ceramic pigments or glazes directly onto starch covered paper or commercial decal paper. To ensure proper coverage of the glazes to be screened, and to preserve the screen as well, it is important that these materials be ground to a finer mesh than the screen. For instance, if a 130-mesh screen is used, then the glaze must be 140-mesh or finer to pass through. The materials can either be purchased in fine grinds or dry ground in a ball mill or with mortar and pestle.

Instead of mixing the glazes with water, better results can be obtained if a medium of equal parts of Damar varnish, boiled linseed oil and turpentine is used. The glaze is added

to the medium until a thick creamy consistency is reached. An alternative mixture of about 40 percent glaze to 60 percent commercial silkscreen medium can also be used.

The image is printed on the prepared paper in the usual manner. As soon as the image dries, a thin coat of varnish or clear acrylic paint is applied to the entire surface. This combines with and bonds the ceramic materials. When the paper is soaked, the starch dissolves and releases the coated image. This is then applied to the ware as a water-mount decal would be.

The ware should dry completely for twenty-four hours before being fired. As with luster glazes, the oxidation firing should start slowly with the door ajar until a temperature of about 450°C (842°F) is reached. The door can then be closed and the firing continued in a strong oxidizing atmosphere until maturing temperature. Most decals mature in the cone 020 to cone 018, (625°-696°C, 1157°-1285°F) range although some manufacturers recommend temperatures as high as cone 014 (834°C, 1533°F). Studio-made decals should, of course, be fired to their particular maturing temperatures, depending on which glaze materials have been used.

8-11

8-12

125

Although underglaze decals are used extensively in industry, few studio potters have experimented with this method to date. The process is basically the same except that the decal is applied to bisque ware which is then glazed and fired to maturity.

Acrylic Lift

This method is an easy way to mount pictures obtained from newspapers or magazines. First, blot denatured alcohol on the chosen picture to loosen the ink. **8-13,** When this has dried, spray or brush five or six coats of clear acrylic paint over the surface. After the paint has dried completely, soak the picture in room temperature water for a half hour. **8-14,** Then remove it and gently rub off all the paper fibers, leaving only the ink impregnated in the acrylic. The acrylic image film can then be secured to a glaze fired object.

Apply a thin coat of acrylic paint to the surface of the object. When this coating becomes tacky, smooth the acrylic image into position and press out any air bubbles.

8-13

8-14

8-15

Cover the image film with one or two thin coats of acrylic paint and let dry. The process is now complete with no additional firing. **8-15,** The disadvantage with this process is that the image can be scratched off.

A somewhat different method can be employed to make an acrylic positive film for photo silkscreen. As before, the chosen image is first blotted with denatured alcohol to loosen the ink. Next, cover a sheet of acetate with a thin coating of clear acrylic paint. Place the picture face down on the acetate and squeegee it on securely. After the acrylic has dried for at least an hour, soak the acetate in room temperature water for a half hour. Gentle rubbing will then remove all the paper fiber, leaving only the ink impregnated in the acetate. When the acetate is dry, it is ready to be used as a positive film in the photo silkscreen process.

Photo Silkscreen

The easiest way to acquire the necessary halftone photo silkscreen image is to take the desired positive or negative to a commercial printer and have it produced and screen mounted.

One method of producing a photo silkscreen in the studio is the Ammonium Bichromate Process. First, prepare at least two screens (one for a test) by tightly stretching and tacking or stapling swatches of 16-denier nylon onto sturdy wooden frames. Roughen the nylon surface with fine sandpaper. Then wash the screen well and allow it to dry.

Under darkroom conditions prepare a formula of 1/4 teaspoon ammonium bichromate, 3 ounces distilled water and 3/4 ounce photo emulsion (Screen Star Photo Emulsion Bond #71 or equivalent). Apply a thin coat of this formula to the screen with a squeegee and let dry. Apply a second thin coat and let it dry.

If a commercially prepared halftone is to be used, simply place it face down on the screen. If an acrylic lift acetate is to be used, place it face down on the screen and place a 90-or 130-mesh halftone transparency sheet on top of it. The image sheet is then covered with a clean piece of glass to keep it flat and in full contact with the emulsion surface.

To make a test screen exposure, first cover the screen with a cardboard. A 500 watt photoflood set 18 inches from the screen is turned on for a minimum of 3 minutes. By moving the board a few inches every 30 seconds, make a series of exposures. Remove the glass and image sheet. Wash the screen in cold water until a faint image is apparent. This may take from 2 to 15 minutes. When the screen is dry, it is ready to be printed. Choose the best exposure time for the final screen and prepare it accordingly.

An alternative method is to use a photosensitized film, such as McGraw 4571 or its equivalent, along with A and B developer. In a darkroom, place the film sticky side down on a piece of clean glass. Put the chosen negative shiny side up on the film and place another piece of glass on top. Place a piece of cardboard over this. Make test strips by exposing sections of the film under a sunlamp at 30 second intervals for a total of at least four minutes. Dark glasses should be worn to protect the eyes. Remove the negative and place the film smooth side down on a piece of glass. Develop for two minutes and wash the film well. If the image is distinct, carefully touch the screen down onto the sticky side of the film. Blot with crumpled newspaper to force the gel to stick to the screen. When the film color no longer comes off onto the newspaper, stop blotting and let the screen dry for 24 hours. Peel off the film backing and the screen is ready to print.

Printing glazes or ceramic pigments with a photo silkscreen is accomplished in the same manner as described in the section on printing decals.

Photo silkscreens can be used to print underglaze decorations on raw or bisque ware and overglaze decorations on fired engobes or glazes. The silkscreen obviously works best on flat or slight single curve surfaces because the wooden frame does not bend. If photo silkscreen prints are desired on curved surfaces, the images can be printed onto decal paper and applied with that technique.

After the printed images have completely dried, the ware can be fired to the maturing temperature of the glazes used.

The screen should be washed with kerosene and a soft toothbrush after each printing session.

8-16 Les Lawrence
Bowl
Thrown stoneware,
   silkscreen transfer decoration
18 x 8 inches
Photo: Kay Colby

8-16

Photoresist

Photoresist on glaze fired ceramics has undergone successful experimentation in at least three versions. One method involves a contact printed positive transparency, the second uses a projected positive transparency, and the third, a projected negative.

Contact Transparency Method This version works best on flat surfaces. Under darkroom conditions, a positive transparency is prepared from a black and white negative by exposure on Contrast Process Film. The negative is focused through an enlarger to the size of the print desired. Close the lens to its smallest aperture and expose the image. A typical exposure might be 10 seconds at f/16. Test strips should be made to arrive at the best time for the particular negative. Develop the film in Kodak DK 50 for 4 minutes, fix, wash, and dry. Other methods of making positive transparencies can also be used.

Printing the transparency is accomplished under yellow safelight conditions in a well ventilated darkroom. A coating of Kodak Photo Resist is brushed or sprayed on glaze fired ware and dried either in a heating oven or by a small fan. A second coating is applied and dried. The transparency is placed face up in close contact with the dry resist surface by taping edges and placing small weights on the darkest areas of the print. The picture is then exposed to a sunlamp or other ultraviolet light source. Eyes should always be protected when using ultraviolet lamps. A typical exposure with a 275 watt sunlamp is about 8 or 10 minutes at 12 inches. Make test strip exposures at 2-minute intervals to find the time best suited for the particular transparency.

To develop the image, ceramic overglazes are mixed with normal N-butyl acetate to a creamy consistency. The mixture is then brushed over the exposed emulsion. Development is instantaneous. Allow the surface to dry completely and then sponge off excess pigment under running water. Edges can be cleaned and image areas lightened with acetone.

Dry the ware completely and then fire to the proper temperature. Commercial overglazes offer the best results, but underglazes fired to cone 04 (1050°C, 1922°F) or oxides fired to cone 6 (1201°C, 2194°F) or above can be mixed with the developer as well.

Projected Positive Transparency Method This version allows a positive transparency image to be used on curved forms. Under red safelight conditions, a thin coat of Kodak Ortho Resist is brushed or sprayed on glaze fired ware.

Because KOR is oxygen sensitive, only small amounts should be used at one time. Dry the ware well in a heating oven.

A regular tungsten light such as that in a slide projector or photo enlarger is used for projecting the transparency onto the sensitized surface. A typical exposure for a 500 watt bulb is about 4 minutes at 12 inches. Test strips should be made for best time with the particular image.

The image is developed by brushing or pouring on a mixture of n-butyl acetate and ceramic overglaze or pigment. KOR emulsion is soft, so care should be taken to prevent scratching. Dry the emulsion thoroughly and then sponge off excess pigment under running water. Clean with acetone if necessary and dry the ware completely before firing to the required temperature of the glaze used.

Projected Negative Method In this method, the need for a positive transparency is avoided. Processing occurs much like normal darkroom methods.

A special photoemulsion is prepared under red safelight conditions in the following manner. In a glass container, 10 grams of gelatin is dissolved in 360 cc of warm water. Add 32 grams of potassium bromide and 0.8 grams of potassium iodide and dissolve. Heat to 55°C (131°F) and hold at that temperature.

Dissolve 40 grams of silver nitrate in 400 cc. of water and slowly add to the potassium bromide solution, maintaining temperature and constantly stirring. Add 40 grams of gelatin to set the emulsion and allow to cool for 3 to 4 hours. When jelled, the emulsion is shredded through cheesecloth into 3 liters of room temperature water. Let stand for 3 minutes and then pour off the water. Repeat four or five times to wash away any soluble salts. Wash the emulsion under running water for 15 minutes and drain. The emulsion can then be refrigerated in a light proof container until it is needed.

The photoemulsion is used in this manner: Under red safelight, heat the emulsion to 55°C (131°F) in a glass beaker, then cool it to 40°C (104°F) and hold at that temperature. Apply the emulsion evenly over the ware by brushing, pouring, or spraying. Dry it completely. Using a red filter on an enlarger, project the negative on the ware for focus and position. Shut off the enlarger and remove the filter. Make a normal print exposure test strip to find the best time for the negative in use. A typical exposure might be f/8 for 20 seconds at 12 inches. Develop in Dektol for about 2 minutes, fix, and then wash in cool water for 10 minutes. After the ware has completely dried, edges can be cleaned by using household bleach. The dry ware is then fired to 866°C (1591°F).

8-17 Malcolm Cochran
Self Portrait
Molded earthenware,
   unfired photo emulsion
12 inches high

8-18 Victor Spinski
Hoover Commemorative Form
Thrown, slab-built and
   molded earthenware, luster glaze,
   fired photo emulsion
26 x 11 1/2 x 2 1/4 inches

8-19 Author
Plate
Thrown stoneware, luster glaze,
   Picceramic photo emulsion process
13 inch diameter

8-17

8-18

8-19

CHAPTER 9 Glazes

An unfired glaze is a dry mixture of powdered inorganic materials which, when heated, will melt to form a viscous liquid. Upon cooling, this liquid hardens into a glassy condition. For ease of application, the unfired glaze is usually mixed in water to make a reasonably stable suspension.

Fired glaze is used primarily for its decorative effects. A glaze can also render a ceramic object nearly impervious to liquids and acids, giving it practical utility, provide a protective coating against weathering and discoloration, and can give additional strength. A fired glaze is very much like a thin layer of glass fused to a ceramic surface which has the chemical and physical characteristics of bottle or window glass.

Obsidian is an example of glass occurring in nature. It is formed by volcanic action which intensely heats minerals within the earth. The molten material is then expelled and slowly cools, forming glass. Man-made glass is also composed of earth materials. It consists of about 75 percent pure sand or silica (SiO_2) and fluxing materials, such as soda ash ($Na_2O \cdot CO_2$) and limestone ($CaO \cdot CO_2$). The addition of fluxes reduces the temperature required to melt the sand from about $1750°C$ ($3182°F$) to less than $1500°C$ ($2732°F$), and reduces the softening temperature of the refined glass to about $1000°C$ ($1832°F$).

The useful properties of a glaze, however, must be quite different from window or bottle glass. An unfired glaze must be able to stay suspended in water for a reasonable time without dissolving. It must be ground fine enough to mix dry without cracking on a ceramic surface, and remain hard enough to allow handling without damage before firing. While in the kiln, the glaze must have a composition that will mature satisfactorily at the desired temperature. After firing, the glaze must cool to fit the ceramic form without cracking or splintering. Of course, the glaze should also look and feel pleasing.

To accomplish all these ends, a glaze must be carefully compounded from a number of ingredients, each serving an important part in the performance of the glaze. Because every one of these materials has its own particular qualities which can react favorably or unfavorably in a glaze, it is necessary to know these properties before attempting to formulate a glaze. A complete listing of raw materials, useful in ceramic glazes, will be found in Appendix A.

Before describing how a glaze is formulated, a few words may be necessary to explain how chemistry is involved in the design of a glaze. Elements combine with one another to form compounds in exact, but simple multiples. For example, one atom of silicon (Si) will combine with two atoms of oxygen (O) to form one molecule of silica (SiO_2). One molecule of soda (Na_2O), one molecule of alumina (Al_2O_3), and 6 molecules of silica (SiO_2) will combine with one another to form one complex molecule of a feldspar ($Na_2O \cdot Al_2O_3 \cdot 6SiO_2$). Because of a difference in the structure of its atoms, the unit weight of each element is different from every other. Consequently, each element has a different atomic weight. Therefore, when 1 atom of silicon combines with 2 atoms of oxygen, 28 parts by weight of silicon combine with 2 x 16 or 32 parts by weight of oxygen to form 60 parts by weight of silica. A chart of atomic weights of common elements and their oxides will be found in Appendix B.

Molecular (Empirical) Formula

For many years, the standard convention for showing how oxide compounds relate to each other in a glaze has been the *molecular formula*, sometimes referred to as the *empirical formula*.

The following table illustrates this grouping of the more common elements used in a glaze. The materials in the RO column are considered bases; those in the R_2O_3 column as amphoteric or neutral in reaction; and those in the RO_2 column as acids. In the molecular formula, glazes are composed under three headings with R expressing the elemental part of the material and O, the oxygen content. The RO materials are the fluxes required to bring about a melt, the R_2O_3 materials are modifiers that affect glaze activity and the RO_2 materials are the glass formers or opacifiers.

RO Bases		R_2O_3 Neutrals	RO_2 Acids
BaO	MgO	Al_2O_3	SiO_2
CaO	MnO	B_2O_3	TiO_2
CdO	Na_2O	Fe_2O_3	ZrO_2 ⎫ opacifiers
FeO	PbO	Sb_2O_3	SnO_2 ⎭
K_2O	SrO	Cr_2O_3	
Li_2O	ZnO		

In the molecular formula, the amounts of the various oxides are expressed in *moles* which represent the *relative number of molecules* present and not their weight. This is done to change the formula into a usable recipe. The **Calculation Formula** of the glaze constituents to be used and the **Equivalent Weight** of the oxides they contain are made to correspond to this mole relationship. The equivalent weight is the weight of the raw material needed in a glaze to give one molecule of the oxide when fired. The calculation formulas and equivalent weights of compounds used in glazing are listed in Appendix C. It should be noted that with most materials, the equivalent weight equals the molecular weight of the raw formula. In some cases, because the compound gains or loses atoms in firing, the equivalent weight will differ. Always use the adjusted equivalent weight when calculating the molecular formula.

To have the molecular formula operate correctly, an arbitrary convention must be used—*that of making the moles in the RO column add up to one, or unity.* This aids in noting the relationship of the fluxes to the amount of silica present in a glaze. It also offers a convenient way to organize the calculation.

A Simple Glaze

As an example, suppose one desires a simple low temperature lead glaze which contains a small amount of zinc oxide to improve transparency. A portion of alumina, or neutral material, is needed to control the glaze flow and devitrification. Sufficient silica, or acid, is needed to cause a good melt. A glaze formula is set up this way:

Bases	Neutrals	Acids
PbO .8	Al_2O_3 .3	SiO_2 1.45
ZnO .2		

To turn this into an actual batch recipe, raw materials must be chosen which will supply the oxides necessary to fulfill the glaze formula. One way to do this would be to use white lead to supply the lead oxide, zinc oxide as the source of zinc oxide, clay for all of the alumina and some of the silica, and flint to give the remaining silica. In their unfired state, many compounds contain water and carbon which are driven off when fired. Other materials contained in the raw formula may also be totally or partially burned out. To make glaze formulation less complicated, some chemical actions are simply disregarded. To avoid confusion, the choice of a glaze material should always be based on its **Calculation Formula** and its corresponding **Equivalent Weight**.

The calculation for this example is set up in a chart as follows: Arrange the oxides in the glaze formula in the top horizontal row with their moles listed directly beneath them. Arrange the chosen raw materials in a vertical row along with their calculation formulas. Fill in the mole of each material needed to fulfill those required in the glaze formula.

Note that the calculation formula for clay calls for one molecule of alumina and two of silica. Therefore the amount of available silica molecules is twice that of alumina and must be so designated in the chart. Add each column of figures and check the totals against the required moles in the glaze formula.

			Oxides in Formula	PbO	ZnO	Al_2O_3	SiO_2
Material	**Calculation Formula**	**Moles**	**Moles in Formula**	.8	.2	.3	1.45
White Lead	PbO	.8		.8			
Zinc Oxide	ZnO	.2			.2		
Clay	$Al_2O_3 \cdot 2SiO_2$	.3				.3	.60
Flint	SiO_2	.85					.85
			Total	.8	.2	.3	1.45

132

After the needed moles are fulfilled in the chart, multiply the mole of each raw material by its equivalent weight to derive a weight factor.

Material	Moles	X	Equivalent Weight	=	Weight Factor
White Lead	.8	x	259	=	207.2
Zinc Oxide	.2	x	81	=	16.2
Clay	.3	x	258	=	77.4
Flint	.85	x	60	=	51.0
					351.8

One additional step should be taken to make the weight factors into a percentage batch. To do this, divide the total weight factor into 100 to derive a key:

$$100 \div 351.8 = .2843$$

Multiply all the weight factors by this key.

Material	Weight Factor	X	Key	=	Percentage Batch
White Lead	207.2	x	.2843	=	58.906
Zinc Oxide	16.2	x	.2843	=	4.605
Clay	77.4	x	.2843	=	22.004
Flint	51.0	x	.2843	=	14.499
					100.014

The percentage batch will give the correct proportion of each compound needed to mix a glaze of any amount. For ease in weighing, amounts in the percentage batch can be arbitrarily rounded off to an exact total of 100.

To solve the following problems, use simple oxide compounds.

Problem A

K_2O	.4	Al_2O_3	.35	SiO_2	2.5
Na_2O	.4				
CaO	.2				

Problem B

Na_2O	.3	Al_2O_3	.38	SiO_2	4.3
BaO	.3				
CaO	.2				
ZnO	.2				

Solutions to the problems will be found in Appendix E.

A Complex Glaze

Even if a more complex glaze is desired for a better surface and melt, the batch is calculated from the glaze formula in the same manner as before. Care must be taken to properly fulfill all the requirements of the glaze formula.

K_2O	.30	Al_2O_3	.35	SiO_2	2.75
CaO	.45				
BaO	.25				

Choose each material from the raw materials chart by its calculation formula. The calcium oxide can be fulfilled by whiting, and the barium oxide by barium carbonate. Although a number of compounds containing potassium oxide could be chosen, in this example the pure potash feldspar, microcline, is used. Its formula is $K_2O \cdot Al_2O_3 \cdot 6SiO_2$, and it has an equivalent weight of 556.

Set up a chart and fulfill needed moles by a raw material.

Note that in the case of microcline there is 6 times the amount of silica as there is potash. Therefore its mole is 6 times .3, or 1.8. With clay, the silica is 2 times .05, or .10. See chart on page 134.

After correctly filling the chart, multiply the moles by their equivalent weights to find the weight factors. Then derive the key and multiply all the weight factors to find the percentage batch.

Material	Moles	X	Equivalent Weight	=	Weight Factor	X	Key	=	% Batch
Microcline	.30	x	556	=	166.80	x	.3077	=	51.324
Whiting	.45	x	100	=	45.00	x	.3077	=	13.846
Barium Carbonate	.25	x	197	=	49.25	x	.3077	=	15.154
Clay	.05	x	258	=	12.90	x	.3077	=	3.969
Flint	.85	x	60	=	51.00	x	.3077	=	15.692
				$100 \div 324.95 = .3077$					99.985

Material	Calculation Formula	Moles	Oxides in Formula Moles in Formula	K_2O	CaO	BaO	Al_2O_3	SiO_2
				.30	.45	.25	.35	2.75
Microcline	$K_2O\cdot Al_2O_3\cdot 6SiO_2$	.30		.30			.30	1.80
Whiting	CaO	.45			.45			
Barium Carbonate	BaO	.25				.25		
Clay	$Al_2O_3\cdot 2SiO_2$	.05					.05	.10
Flint	SiO_2	.85						.85
			Total	.30	.45	.25	.35	2.75

To solve the following problem use anorthite as the feldspar.

Problem C

CaO .3	Al_2O_3 .34	SiO_2 2.60
Na_2O .3		
BaO .2		
MgO .1		
ZnO .1		

To solve the following problem use albite as the feldspar and dolomite as the source of magnesium oxide.

Problem D

Na_2O .4	Al_2O_3 .45	SiO_2 3.4
CaO .3		
MgO .2		
BaO .1		

Solutions will be found in Appendix E.

A More Complex Glaze

The following formula is typical of a glaze which calls for a compound that appears to have oxides in amounts greater than can be used.

PbO .5	Al_2O_3 .25	SiO_2 1.80
CaO .3	B_2O_3 .30	
ZnO .2		

White lead and zinc oxide can supply the needed lead and zinc oxides. Colemanite can be used to supply both the calcium oxide and boron. Whiting, clay and flint will also be needed.

If colemanite is used to fulfill all the calcium oxide it will contribute more boron to the formula than can be used. Instead, the colemanite will be thought of as supplying all the boron and only some of the calcium oxide. The following ratio will derive the needed amount:

$$\frac{\text{What is needed in the formula}}{\text{What is present in the material}} = \text{amount to be used}$$

Therefore, to find the amount of colemanite to be used in the example:

$$\frac{.3 \quad B_2O_3}{1.5 \quad B_2O_3} = .2 \text{ mole of colemanite}$$

Multiply all the oxides in colemanite by .2 and insert these moles in the chart. All the boron is now satisfied along with most of the calcium oxide. Whiting will fill the remaining calcium oxide. Clay and flint complete the formula.

The batch is calculated as follows:

			Oxides in Formula	PbO	CaO	ZnO	B₂O₃	Al₂O₃	SiO₂
Material	Calculation Formula	Moles	Moles in Formula	.5	.3	.2	.3	.25	1.8
White Lead	PbO	.5		.5					
Colemanite	CaO·1.5B₂O₃	.2			.2		.3		
Whiting	CaO	.1			.1				
Zinc Oxide	ZnO	.2				.2			
Clay	Al₂O₃·2SiO₂	.25						.25	.5
Flint	SiO₂	1.3							1.3
			Total	.5	.3	.2	.3	.25	1.8

Material	Moles	X	Equivalent Weight	=	Weight Factor	X	Key	=	% Batch
White Lead	.5	x	259	=	129.5	x	.2946	=	38.151
Colemanite	.2	x	206	=	41.2	x	.2946	=	12.138
Whiting	.1	x	100	=	10.0	x	.2946	=	2.946
Zinc Oxide	.2	x	81	=	16.2	x	.2946	=	4.773
Clay	.25	x	258	=	64.5	x	.2946	=	19.002
Flint	1.3	x	60	=	78.0	x	.2946	=	22.979

$$100 \div 339.4 = .2946$$

99.989

The derived amount ratio is also required when a complex feldspar is to be used in a glaze formula.

In the example the feldspar used has an equivalent weight of 571 and the formula:

Na₂O	.18	Al₂O₃	.38	SiO₂	2.50
K₂O	.10				
CaO	.23				
ZnO	.26				
BaO	.23				

Na₂O	.50	Al₂O₃	1.01	SiO₂	6.65
K₂O	.28				
CaO	.22				

To use the feldspar, divide the amount of Na_2O in the glaze formula by the Na_2O in the feldspar to find its mole.

$$\frac{.18}{.50} = .36 \text{ mole of feldspar}$$

Multiply each oxide in the feldspar by .36 and insert the number in its proper column.

Whiting is used for the remainder of the calcium oxide. Zinc oxide and barium carbonate fulfill their formula requirements. Clay and flint fill the needed alumina and silica.

Material	Calculation Formula	Moles	Moles in Formula	Na_2O	K_2O	CaO	ZnO	BaO	Al_2O_3	SiO_2
			Oxides in Formula	.18	.10	.23	.26	.23	.38	2.50
Spar	$Na_2O.50Al_2O_3 1.01\ SiO_2 6.65$ $K_2O.28$ $CaO.22$	.36		.18	.10	.08			.36	2.39
Whiting	CaO	.15				.15				
Zinc Oxide	ZnO	.26					.26			
Barium Carbonate	BaO	.23						.23		
Clay	$Al_2O_3 \cdot 2SiO_2$	.02							.02	.04
Flint	SiO_2	.07								.07
			Total	.18	.10	.23	.26	.23	.38	2.50

Material	Moles	X	Equivalent Weight	=	Weight Factor	X	Key	=	% Batch
Feldspar	.36	x	571	=	205.56	x	.3375	=	69.377
Whiting	.15	x	100	=	15.00	x	.3375	=	5.063
Zinc Oxide	.26	x	81	=	21.06	x	.3375	=	7.108
Barium Carbonate	.23	x	197	=	45.31	x	.3375	=	15.292
Clay	.02	x	258	=	5.16	x	.3375	=	1.742
Flint	.07	x	60	=	4.20	x	.3375	=	1.418

$$100 \div 296.29 = .3375$$

100.00

To solve the following formula use borax.

Problem E

Na₂0	.3	Al₂O₃	.2	SiO₂	3.4
PbO	.4	B₂O₃	.35		
ZnO	.2				
BaO	.1				

To solve the following formula use Kona F-4 feldspar.

Problem F

Na₂O	.27	Al₂O₃	.56	SiO₂	4.60
K₂O	.17				
CaO	.24				
ZnO	.15				
BaO	.17				

The solutions will be found in Appendix E.

To Find a Glaze Formula from a Batch

Sometimes it is necessary to take a batch recipe and return it to its glaze formula. This is important when a glaze material becomes unavailable and a substitution is needed, when comparing two glazes, or if a glaze does not fire properly.

To find a glaze formula from a batch, divide the percentage batch weight of each material by its equivalent weight.

Material	Batch	÷	Equivalent Weight	=	Mole Factor
White Lead (PbO)	58.80	÷	259	=	.227
Zinc Oxide (ZnO)	4.60	÷	81	=	.057
Clay (Al₂O₃·2SiO₂)	22.06	÷	258	=	.086
Flint (SiO₂)	14.54	÷	60	=	.242

Write this as a formula. Note that clay has twice the silica as alumina. Therefore, multiply .086 by 2 for the correct amount of silica and add it into the SiO₂ total.

PbO	.227	Al₂O₃	.086	SiO₂	.242
ZnO	.057				+.172
	.284				.414

To make the RO column equal one, or unity, divide its sum into 1 to get the key.

$$1 \div .284 = 3.521$$

Multiply all the glaze constituents by the key to derive the correct formula.

PbO	.227	x	3.521	=	.799
ZnO	.057	x	3.521	=	.200
Al₂O₃	.086	x	3.521	=	.303
SiO₂	.414	x	3.521	=	1.458

The figures may be rounded off and put into a glaze formula.

PbO	.8	Al₂O₃	.3	SiO₂	1.46
ZnO	.2				

The same method is used to write the formula of a more complex glaze batch. In the example, albite is used as the feldspar. Its formula is Na₂O·Al₂O₃·6SiO₂ and it has an equivalent weight of 524.

First, divide the batch weight of each material by its equivalent weight to find its mole.

Material	Batch	÷	Equivalent Weight	=	Mole Factor
Albite	52.9	÷	524	=	.101
Whiting	11.2	÷	100	=	.112
Barium Carbonate	12.7	÷	197	=	.064
Zinc Oxide	3.8	÷	81	=	.047
Clay	4.2	÷	258	=	.016
Flint	15.2	÷	60	=	.253

Arrange all the oxides horizontally in a chart with all the raw materials and their calculation formulas vertically. Fill in the mole factors.

Note that the SiO₂ in albite is 6 times the Na₂O and in clay it is 2 times the Al₂O₃.

Material	Calculation Formula	Moles	Oxides in Formula	Na$_2$O	CaO	BaO	ZnO	Al$_2$O$_3$	SiO$_2$
Albite	Na$_2$O·Al$_2$O$_3$·6SiO$_2$	.101		.101				.101	.606
Whiting	CaO	.112			.112				
Barium Carbonate	BaO	.064				.064			
Zinc Oxide	ZnO	.047					.047		
Clay	Al$_2$O$_3$·2SiO$_2$	.016						.016	.032
Flint	SiO$_2$	.253							.253
			Total	.101	.112	.064	.047	.117	.891

Add the numbers in each oxide column and arrange the totals in a formula.

Na$_2$O	.101	Al$_2$O$_3$	.117	SiO$_2$	.891
CaO	.112				
BaO	.064				
ZnO	.047				
	.324				

Divide the sum of the RO column into 1 to get the key.

$$1 \div .324 = 3.086$$

Multiply each oxide by the key to derive a unity formula.

Na$_2$O	.101	x	3.086	=		.3116
CaO	.112	x	3.086	=		.3456
BaO	.064	x	3.086	=		.1975
ZnO	.047	x	3.086	=		.1450
Al$_2$O$_3$	.117	x	3.086	=		.3610
SiO$_2$	.891	x	3.086	=		2.7496

The equivalents may be rounded off and arranged in a glaze formula.

Na$_2$O	.31	Al$_2$O$_3$	.36	SiO$_2$	2.75
CaO	.35				
BaO	.20				
ZnO	.15				
	1.01				

Problem G

White Lead	46.4
Whiting	9.3
Zinc Oxide	2.4
Clay	19.4
Flint	22.5

Problem H

Nepheline Syenite	45.3
Whiting	9.7
Barium Carbonate	23.2
Zinc Oxide	8.8
Clay	13.0

The solutions will be found in Appendix E.

Limit Formulas

The following table lists the approximate effective range of the amount of an oxide which can be used in a glaze at a given temperature. Use the information as a general guide. It can be helpful in constructing a new glaze or correcting a faulty one. Remember that in practice the RO column must equal *one*.

C/08-04   (945°-1050°C/1733°-1922°F)   **Lead Glazes**

PbO	.2 - .6	Al_2O_3	.15 - .2	SiO_2	1.5 - 2.5
KNaO	.1 - .25	B_2O_3	.15 - .6		
ZnO	.1 - .25				
CaO	.3 - .6				
BaO	0 - .15				

C/08-04   (945°-1050°C/1733°-1922°F)   **Alkaline Glazes**

PbO	0 - .5	Al_2O_3	.05 - .25	SiO_2	1.5 - 2.5
KNaO	.4 - .8				
CaO	0 - .3				
ZnO	0 - .2				

C/2-5   (1142°-1177°C/2088°-2151°F)   **Lead Glazes**

PbO	.4 - .6	Al_2O_3	.2 - .28	SiO_2	2.0 - 3.0
KNaO	.1 - .25				
CaO	.1 - .4				
ZnO	0 - .25				

C/2-5   (1142°-1177°C/2088°-2151°F)   **Colemanite Glazes**

KNaO	.1 - .3	Al_2O_3	.2 - .35	SiO_2	2.0 - 3.0
CaO	.2 - .5	B_2O_3	.3 - .6		
ZnO	.1 - .25				
BaO	.1 - .25				

C/8-12   (1236°-1306°C/2257°-2383°F)   **Stoneware Glazes**

KNaO	.2 - .4	Al_2O_3	.3 - .5	SiO_2	3.0 - 5.0
CaO	.4 - .7				
ZnO	0 - .3	B_2O_3	.1 - .3		
BaO	0 - .3				
MgO	0 - .35				
Li_2O	0 - .3				

Chemical Analysis of a Feldspar to Formula

To accurately use a feldspar in a glaze formula it is necessary to know its formula and equivalent weight. A feldspar comes from the manufacturer with a percentage analysis which must be made into a calculation formula.
   Suppose a feldspar has the following analysis:

SiO_2	50.63%
Al_2O_3	27.00
K_2O	13.20
Na_2O	9.10
LOI (loss on ignition)	.07

Divide the percentage of each compound by its atomic weight to derive its mole factor. For simplification, loss on ignition is discarded.

Material	Percentage	÷	Atomic Weight	=	Mole Factor
SiO_2	50.63	÷	60	=	.844
Al_2O_3	27.00	÷	102	=	.265
K_2O	13.20	÷	94	=	.140
Na_2O	9.10	÷	62	=	.147

Set up these figures as a formula.

K_2O	.140	Al_2O_3	.265	SiO_2	.844
Na_2O	.147				
	.287				

To derive a unity formula, add the RO column and then divide that sum into 1 to find the key.

$$1 \div .287 = 3.484$$

139

Multiply each oxide by the key and arrange the answers as a formula.

K$_2$O   .49   Al$_2$O$_3$ .92   SiO$_2$ 2.94
Na$_2$O   .51

To derive the equivalent weight of the feldspar, multiply the moles by their atomic weights and add the weight factors.

Material	Moles	X	Atomic Weight	=	Weight Factor
K$_2$O	.49	x	94	=	46.06
Na$_2$O	.51	x	62	=	31.62
Al$_2$O$_3$	.92	x	102	=	93.84
SiO$_2$	2.94	x	60	=	176.40
	Equivalent weight of feldspar			=	347.92 or 348

Problem I		Problem J	
SiO$_2$	66.3%	SiO$_2$	67.10%
Al$_2$O$_3$	18.4	Al$_2$O$_3$	19.10
CaO	.4	CaO	.94
Na$_2$O	2.7	Na$_2$O	6.56
K$_2$O	11.8	K$_2$O	5.91
LOI	.4	LOI	.39

Solutions will be found in Appendix E.

To Calculate from Glaze Formula to Percentage Batch

1. Construct a chart showing oxides in formula and their moles horizontally with raw materials and their calculation formulas vertically.
2. If alkalies are present, fill in feldspar moles.
3. Fill single oxide moles—other than silica.
4. Fill two-oxide moles—other than alumina and silica.
5. Fill remaining alumina with clay.
6. Fill remaining silica with flint.
7. Multiply all moles by their equivalent weights to find the weight factors.
8. Derive key by dividing total weight factor into 100.
9. Use key to derive percentage batch weight.

To Calculate from Percentage Batch to Glaze Formula

1. Divide the percentage batch weight of each material by its equivalent weight to derive moles.
2. Arrange all the oxides in a chart horizontally with the raw materials and their calculation formulas vertically.
3. Fill in the moles.
4. With complex materials, multiply the amount of each oxide by its mole and record the answers.
5. Add each oxide column.
6. Arrange the totals as a formula.
7. Derive key by dividing the sum of the RO column into 1.
8. Bring the formula to unity by using key.

By using the foregoing calculations, a glaze can be formulated from scratch or altered to correct firing problems; new materials can be substituted; or glazes can be accurately compared with each other. The only true test of the worth of a glaze is in its firing.

To mix a glaze, weigh the raw materials separately. Dry mix them and then add water until the mixture has a consistency of light cream. Screen the glaze through a 50- or 60-mesh sieve for smoothness. If the glaze is too thick, add more water and rescreen. If the glaze is too thin, let it settle and then siphon off the excess water.

Colorants

Colorants and opacifiers are normally introduced into a glaze as percentage additions. The following chart should be used only as a suggested guide for the amount of an oxide needed to color a glaze. In practice the actual color depends on the compounds in the base glaze, the particle size, purity and concentration of the colorant, atmospheric conditions, and the temperature to which the ware is fired. Colors on white clay will appear brighter than on dark clay.

Temperatures up to cone 010 (887°C, 1629°F) should be considered very low; those from cone 09 to cone 06 (915-991°C, 1679-1816°F) considered as low; from cone 05 to cone 6 (1031-1201°C, 1888-2194°F) as medium; and temperatures above cone 7 (1215°C, 2219°F), high.

Color	Oxide	Percentage	Temperature	Atmosphere
Red				
	Chrome—tin (1:5)—pink	1—2	all	oxidation
	Chrome (high PbO)—coral	5	very low	oxidation
	Iron (high SiO_2, KNaO)	2—5	low	oxidation
	Iron	8—12	high	reduction
	Copper	1—3	all	reduction
Orange				
	Uranium (high PbO)	5—8	very low	oxidation
	Selenium (no PbO)	3—4	very low	oxidation
Yellow				
	Antimony yellow stain (high PbO)	3—5	low	both
	Chrome (high PbO, Na_2O)	1	low	oxidation
	Uranium (high PbO)	5—8	very low	oxidation
	Vanadium tin stain	4—6	all	both
	Vanadium zirconium stain	5—10	all	both
	Iron (high Na_2O, BaO)	1—2	high	reduction
Green				
	Copper	1—5	all	oxidation
	Chrome	2—4	low-medium	oxidation
	Nickel (MgO)	3—5	low	oxidation
	Iron—celadon	1—3	all	reduction
Blue				
	Cobalt	1/2—1	all	both
	Copper (high BaO)	2—4	high	oxidation
	Copper (high KNaO)—turquoise	3—5	low	oxidation
	Nickel (ZnO)	1—3	low	oxidation
	Iron (CaO or BaO)	1/2—1	high	reduction
	Nickel (BaO, ZnO)	1—3	high	reduction
Violet				
	Manganese (KNaO or BaO)	4—6	medium	oxidation
Tan				
	Iron (PbO)—amber	2—5	low	oxidation
	Iron	1—2	all	both
	Manganese	2	all	both
	Rutile	2	all	both

(Chart continued on next page)

Color	Oxide	Percentage	Temperature	Atmosphere
Brown				
	Chrome (MgO, ZnO)	2—5	low	both
	Iron	3—7	all	both
	Manganese	5	all	both
	Nickel (ZnO)	2—4	all	both
	Rutile	5	all	reduction
Black				
{	Cobalt	1—2	all	both
{	Manganese	2—4		
{	Cobalt	1	all	both
{	Iron	8		
{	Manganese	3		
Grey				
	Nickel	1—2	all	oxidation
White				
	Tin	5	all	both
	Zirconium	8—12	all	both
	Titanium—blue-white	8—12	all	both
	Antimony—yellow-white	10-12	low	oxidation

Three methods for mixing colorant into glaze can be used: the Line Blend, the 50-50 Dry Blend, and the Tri-axial Blend.

Line Blend

A straight line blend can be used to proportionately combine two colored glazes. As an example, a six-point line is shown.

	①	②	③	④	⑤	⑥	
A	100	80	60	40	20	0	
	0	20	40	60	80	100	**B**

Point 4 is therefore a mixture of 40 percent glaze A and 60 percent glaze B.

142

50-50 Dry Blend

Many more gradations of color can be derived from a single base glaze by combining a number of colorants in a logical manner. For this method flat tiles at least one and one-half inches square need to be made and bisque fired. In an example using five colorants, 21 tiles are needed. Mark them on the back with underglaze pencil or oxide wash as follows:

B	1	2	3	4	5
	B+1	B+2	B+3	B+4	B+5
		1+2	1+3	1+4	1+5
			2+3	2+4	2+5
				3+4	3+5
					4+5

B is the base glaze and numbers 1 to 5 are each a specific percentage of different coloring oxides. Weigh a 100 gram portion of dry base for each colorant and place it in a numbered bag or clean glass jar. Add the percentage of desired colorant to each container except the base container. For instance, three grams of copper carbonate added to one container would be a 3 percent addition of copper. Dry screen the glaze at least three times through a coarse sieve or kitchen strainer to ensure thorough mixing.

To mix a test sample, start with the second row of tiles. Weigh 10 grams from container B and 10 grams from container 1. Grind them together with a spatula on a glass slab, adding water from a syringe. Avoid adding too much water. Dip tile B + 1 in water and then apply the mix with the spatula. When the tile is dry, clean off the edges. Weigh 10 grams from container B and 10 grams from container 2 and mix them. Continue in this manner until all the tiles have been coated with glaze. The top row of tiles is coated with mix directly from each container. When they are dry, fire the samples.

After the tiles are fired, they may be glued to a board in their original positions. To find the amount of oxides needed for a particular color, start at the desired tile and look vertically to the top to find one colorant. Again, starting at the desired tile, look horizontally to the first empty space at the left and then read to the top of that row to find the other. For instance, for tile 2 + 4, the top of the vertical row is colorant 4 and the first horizontal empty space to the left is colorant 2. When mixing the glaze, add to the base one-half the percentage of colorant in row 4 and one-half the percentage of colorant in row 2.

Triaxial Blend

This is a method of choosing a color blend using three oxides. Points along the outer edge are simple line blends of the two constituents on the line. Inner points are read by counting spaces from each line inward. Count the spaces in from line *BC* to get the percentage of *A*; from *AC* to get the percentage of *B*; from *AB* to get *C*.

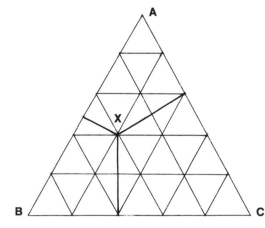

In the example, if each space equals 20 percent, then point *X* would be 40 percent colorant *A*; 40 percent colorant *B*; and 20 percent *C*. These amounts are then weighed and mixed into the base glaze.

9-1 Pitcher
12-13th century Mesopotamian
Egyptian Paste
7 1/2 inches high
Courtesy: Museum of Fine Arts, Boston
    Gift of K. Aharonian

9-2 G. Portanier
Platter
Thrown earthenware, alkaline glaze
16 inch diameter

All three methods can also be used to compound wet mixed colorants provided that the glazes are accurately weighed in 100 cc amounts. Water should be added to the lighter mix until the glazes weigh out equally. Carefully measure each glaze in a graduated cylinder before combining. Shake well and then apply to a tile.

The line blend or the triaxial blend can also be used to formulate a clay body.

Glaze Types

Egyptian Paste   The earliest glazes were apparently developed seven thousand years ago by Egyptians who mixed soluble sodium salts and a bit of copper into their clay. As the clay dried, the salts came to the surface. In the firing, they melted to form a vibrant blue glaze. As time passed, a mixture of soda ash, clay, sand and copper was used instead. The mixture was painted on the surface of an object and then fired at a very low heat.

Low-Fire Alkaline Glaze   An alkaline glaze is fluxed by alkalies such as sodium oxide or potassium oxide. Both active fluxes, soda and potash can cause a glaze to run or craze if overfired or if mixed with too little alumina. Early Mediterranean alkaline glaze tended to craze or peel and was often soluble in food acids. Alkaline glaze has been widely used, however, because it encourages bright yellow and blue colors and melts easily at low temperatures. To overcome the drawback of solubility, most alkaline fluxes are now introduced into a glaze in fritted form.

Lead Glaze   Lead sulfide, or galena, was probably first used as a glaze material by ancient Babylonians. Dusted or painted on a raw pot, the lead would fuse to a shiny glaze when fired. A simple lead glaze is often made with as much as 50 percent of a lead compound. It is more commonly used with other fluxes to improve luster, control glaze melt and develop colors. Low-fire glaze is easily scratched and can take on a dull appearance. Fired above cone 01 (1117°C, 2045°F), a lead glaze becomes more durable. Lead compounds are poisonous but can be more safely introduced

9-1

9-2

into a glaze in fritted form. The use of lead should be kept to a minimum or completely avoided.

Aventurine Glaze Usually a low temperature, high lead base is used for this type of glaze. An addition of seven to twelve percent of iron oxide melts into solution during the heat cycle. As the ware slowly cools, the iron crystallizes on the surface as red or gold crystals. Other low temperature fluxes can be used for varying effects.

Crystalline Glaze Glaze is normally a noncrystalline substance when cooled. The alumina necessary to make a glaze viscous also prevents crystallization. A glaze with little or no alumina will be very runny, but will favor crystal growth. A high zinc content will aid in developing crystals. Rutile or titanium will also help. Alkaline glazes fluxed with lithium are often more successful bases than those fluxed with other materials. Mixing a glaze with liquid silicate instead of water will promote crystals.

For the best crystal development, the kiln is heated to temperature normally, but then rapidly dropped about $38°C$ ($100°F$) and held at that temperature for a few hours before being very slowly cooled. Crystals in a glaze are very elusive and much experimentation with glaze bases, colorants and cooling cycles is often necessary before consistent results can be expected.

Ash Glaze The first ash glaze was probably accidental, caused by wood ash falling on a pot fired in a crude kiln. The composition of natural ash, be it wood, rice hull or other vegetable matter, varies greatly with the material. Ash generally contains from thirty to seventy percent silica, 10 to 15 percent alumina and other materials such as potash, lime or magnesia. Most ash will melt to a watery looking glaze at about cone 10 ($1285°C$, $2345°F$). For better glaze quality, fit and control, ash is usually mixed with small amounts of clay,

9-3

9-4 Elsa Rady
Bottles
Thrown stoneware, crystalline glaze
Tallest: 6 inches high

9-4

145

9-5 David MacAllister
Vase
Thrown stoneware, slip, fly ash
6 inches high

9-6 Jim Hurt
Jar
Thrown stoneware, ash glaze
9 1/2 inches high

9-7 Jug
18th century American
Thrown earthenware, slip glaze
Courtesy: Museum of Art, Rhode Island
School of Design, Providence, R.I.

whiting or feldspar. Before ash is mixed into a glaze, it should be put through a coarse sieve to screen out unburned material. Wear rubber gloves and use a respirator mask because ash is caustic. Dry screening through a 60-mesh sieve will leave soluble salts in the ash, which may be preferred for mottled glaze effects. To remove soluble salts, mix the ash with water and screen through a 60-mesh sieve. Allow the mixture to settle and then siphon out the water, drawing off the soluble materials. A second washing may be desirable. Dry the ash thoroughly before use.

Slip Glaze Many common earthenware clays when fired above cone 8 (1236°C, 2257°F) will melt to a smooth, glossy, brownish glaze. Much Chinese and Colonial American ware was fired with local slip glazes. To test a local clay, simply put a small amount of the dry clay in a bisqued dish and fire to the desired temperature. If it melts completely, it may be used as a glaze without modification. Often a small amount of frit or feldspar will bring about a better melt. Most slip glazes have a two- or three-cone firing range.

Slip is best applied on leather hard ware. This allows the glaze and ware to shrink equally. Otherwise, the glaze may crack in drying and crawl when fired.

9-5

9-6

9-7

9-8 Regis C. Brodie
Bottle
Thrown porcelain, slip glaze, salt glaze
8 inches high

9-9 Elsa Rady
Bowls
Thrown porcelain, carved, fluted,
    crackle glaze
Largest: 5 3/4 x 2 inches

9-10 Author
Raku bowl
5 x 3 inches

Frit Glaze A frit is an artificial fusion of ceramic materials. Fritting renders raw glaze materials nearly insoluble and less toxic. The raw materials, often lead or alkaline fluxes, are melted in a special kiln with silica and other compounds. When the mixture becomes molten, a hole at the bottom of the kiln is opened and the contents run slowly into cold water or onto a cold steel plate. The glass-like nuggets are then dry milled to the desired fineness. It is a time consuming process and the use of commercially available frits is therefore recommended.

Below cone 06 ($991°C$, $1816°F$) many frits function well by themselves as glazes. Additions of clay, flint or whiting will control glaze fit and melt.

Crackle Glaze A crackle glaze is one that has been deliberately made to craze by using oxides with high expansion rates in the glaze base. Most often, crazing is considered a fault, but if properly controlled, it can become effective decoration. To accent the network of fine cracks in a fired glaze, strong tea or carbon ink can be brushed on the ware and then rubbed off. The color seeps into the cracks leaving a web of dark lines. Another way to accent crackle is to rub a coloring oxide into the craze. By refiring the ware to a slightly higher temperature the dark crackle is sealed into the glaze. In raku firing, strong secondary reduction will accent crazed glaze.

Matt Glaze A dull glaze that has been applied thinly or underfired is not a matt glaze. A true matt glaze is fully matured and smooth but without gloss. An excess of barium above .2 moles will change most glazes to matt. Barium tends to form a glass with boron and therefore may not matt a glaze with high B_2O_3. Increased alumina in a glaze makes it more refractory and tends to create a matt surface. A matt glaze may not be good to use on table ware because its tiny crystalline surface structure is hard to clean.

Bristol Glaze Bristol glaze was purportedly developed in nineteenth century England as a substitute for the more dangerous raw lead glaze. Using zinc oxide as the flux, Bristol glazes have been developed from cone 2 ($1142°C$, $2088°F$) to cone 14 ($1388°C$, $2530°F$). The more common firing range is between cone 5 ($1177°C$, $2151°F$) and cone 9 ($1260°C$, $2300°F$). Contrary to popular notion, Bristol glazes are not necessarily stiff, rough, and hard to use. They can be glossy, matt, clear, colored, or opaque depending upon the constituents of the glaze. The general composition of zinc oxide, alkalies, alkaline earths, clay, and silica has a high viscosity which allows a Bristol glaze to mature without running or shifting. Because the glaze is resistant to weathering, abrasion and most acids, it is used to a great extent in architectural ceramics. One drawback is that if the glaze is improperly applied, it could separate and crawl during firing. Bristol glaze is normally used for glazing raw ware and single firing over an extended time up to 50 hours. By substituting calcined zinc and calcined clay, the glaze can be used on bisque fired ware with much less chance of firing faults.

Salt Glaze, Raku, and Reduction Glaze all require special firing and are discussed in Chapter Ten. **Luster Glaze** is discussed in Chapter Eight.

9-8

9-9

9-10

CHAPTER 10 Firing

While it is true that some ancient unfired clay fertility figures and adobe structures have withstood the ravages of time, bone dry clay pieces in contact with water will soon return to their original muddy state. In order to achieve greater strength and permanency, clay must undergo the process of firing. During a firing, many chemical changes take place which permanently alter the state of the clay.

The earliest of these changes is at about 100°C (212°F) when the atmospheric moisture leaves the ware in the form of steam. If this temperature is reached too quickly, the clay will explode. Silica undergoes its first chemical change from alpha cristobalite to beta cristobalite at about 220° to 275°C (428°-527°F). *Water smoking* or evaporation of chemically combined water from the clay, occurs from 450° to 600°C (842°-1112°F). Considerable abrupt shrinkage takes place at this time as kaolinite changes to metakaolin. Therefore, the temperature rise should be gradual to keep the ware from splitting. Silica changes again around 573°C (1063°F) from alpha to beta quartz. By 700°C (1292°F) all organic and inorganic compounds such as carbon and the carbonates have become decomposed or oxidized. At 870°C (1598°F) silica changes once more, this time into its tridymite formation. Another major and sudden shrinkage takes place at 950° to 980°C (1742°-1796°F) when the metakaolin changes to spinel. From 1050° to 1100°C (1922°-2012°F) mullite crystals begin to grow through the combination of alumina and silica, giving the clay its strength. As the temperature continues to rise, more silica slowly forms a glass around the mullite crystals, increasing the hardness of the clay. While the glassy phase continues, further shrinkage takes place at 1200°C (2192°F) when the silica changes to the more complete form of cristobalite.

Impurities and varied composition control the extent of maturation in clay bodies. Iron loaded earthenware clays mature, that is, reach their highest point of favorable vitrification, at about 1090°C (1994°F), while most stonewares mature at 1290°C (2354°F) and pure kaolins mature at about 1650°C (3002°F) or higher.

The cooling cycle of a firing is as critical as the heat rise. If the clay cools too rapidly, remaining uncombined silica inverts, or reverses, its reaction at about 573°C (1063°F) and consequently contracts, causing the ware to crack. Care should therefore be taken to have a slow steady heating and cooling cycle. Such temperature control can be easily regulated by using a well insulated kiln. Although specific types of kilns are discussed in the chapter on Kilns, Wheels, and Studio Equipment, a kiln is basically a container in which clay objects can be heated.

How to safely put ware into a kiln so that it will not be damaged is both a challenge and an art. When loading or stacking a kiln, a supply of kiln shelves and various sized kiln posts should be on hand to allow maximum use of the interior kiln space. For lower temperature work, light weight and fairly inexpensive refractory clay shelves are available. They may be used at higher temperatures around 1260°C (2300°F). If used frequently at this higher range, they can weaken rapidly and fail when least expected. The more expensive silicon carbide shelves, although somewhat brittle, have a higher heat conductivity, heat more evenly throughout, withstand higher temperatures for longer periods of time, and are therefore recommended, particularly for large, fuel burning kilns.

Refractory kiln posts of varied heights can be obtained commercially; hollow types conduct heat better than solid ones. Firebrick *soaps* (9" x 2 1/2" x 2 1/4") can also be used as kiln posts, especially in larger kilns.

The upper surface of kiln shelves should be given a thin, even coating of kiln wash to prevent dripped glaze from permanently sticking after a firing. Equal parts, by weight, of flint and kaolin mixed with water to the consistency of thick paint can be applied with a wide brush or paint roller. Two percent of bentonite added to the dry ingredients before mixing will help prevent the wash from settling in its container and also give a better bond to the shelf. Kiln wash adheres more easily to a shelf that has been warmed than to a cold one. Clean any drippings of wash off the sides and bottom of the shelves before they are used. Rewash the kiln shelves frequently between firings, but do not allow a heavy buildup of wash to occur as this can make the surface uneven and also decrease shelf conductivity. Occasional scraping and wirebrushing of the shelves will prevent this. Never kilnwash the roof or walls of a kiln or the underside of the shelves because flakes of wash might fall into the ware below and spoil the glazes.

Glaze which has stuck to a washed shelf during the firing can be carefully chipped off with a chisel. Keep the chisel at an acute angle to the shelf and tap lightly with a mallet to free the glaze but not break the shelf. If, by chance, an entire pot becomes stuck to the shelf, hold the pot and gently strike the shelf around it with a leather, wood, or rubber mallet. Do not hit the pot because it might break. Keep tapping until the piece can be removed.

Special equipment such as tile setters, plate racks, pins, stilts, and so on are commercially available for specific stacking problems. Generally, these items are not required to fully load a kiln. Tile setters are special nesting refractory racks on which flat tiles can be placed to reduce warping and protect the glazed surface while taking up less space in the kiln than if the tiles were placed singly. **10-1,** Plate racks are usually refractory saggars with porcelain dowels put through the sides to support a number of plates. Pins and stilts, made of high refractory materials, are used to support single pieces which have been totally glazed.

Pyrometric Cones

In the long history of ceramics, the pyrometric cone is a fairly recent development. At first, no method of heat registering was used and luck played a great part in the success or failure of a firing. For many centuries *draw trials* were used. A number of small rings of clay were placed in the kiln near a spy hole. As the temperature increased, rings were periodically removed from the kiln with a long iron hook to check the clay and glaze consistency. **10-2,** Some potters use this method today, often, however, in conjunction with cones.

In the early 1700s Josiah Wedgewood developed the first method for scientific measurement. Because the clay bulk decreases as the firing temperature rises, he was able to put draw trials into a calibrated steel box, checking their shrinkage, until a trial had shrunk to the size he determined to be correctly related to the maturing of his clay.

In the 1880s the German ceramist, Hermann Seger, developed pyramid shaped cones which were made up of controlled clay bodies designed to fuse at specific temperature intervals. Today the full series of cones numbers from cone 022, which is just above red heat, to cone 42. Because there is no international standard regarding temperature scale, there are variations between Seger cones, primarily used in Europe, and Orton cones which come in two sizes and are used in the United States. The Orton cones are designed to measure *heat work*, that is, the time/temperature effect in firing ceramics. There is a temperature variation of $-9.4°C$ ($15°F$) between the small cones and the large cones which are heavier and bend earlier.

Normally, three consecutively numbered large cones are placed side by side in a plaque or pat of clay. The lower temperature, or *guide cone*, is placed to the right, the *desired temperature cone* in the center and a higher, or *guard cone*, to the left. The cones, with their stamped numbers facing right, are set in the clay at an angle of 8 degrees. Small cones set with the numbers facing to the

10-1

10-2

10-3

10-4

side. With a fork, punch holes in the clay pat to allow rapid, even drying and to prevent explosion during the fire. Recently the Orton Foundation has developed a self-supporting cone which eliminates any variation in the setting angle by simply standing it flat on a level kiln shelf.

As each cone nears its fusion point, it begins to soften and bend in the direction of its stamped number. Temperature is generally considered to have been reached when the tip of the cone has bent to the level of the base. After the guide cone has bent, the kiln should be checked at more frequent intervals until the firing cone has fully bent. The heat is then shut off and the kiln allowed to cool slowly. Do not reuse unbent cones because chemical changes have taken place in them which will give incorrect information.

When stacking a kiln, cone pats should be placed so that they do not bend against a pot and can be easily seen through the spy holes of the kiln. For better control of a multilevel electric or large fuel kiln, which often have uneven heat distribution, each spy hole should have its own set of cones. As the heat in the kiln increases, the cones become easier to see because of the interior color of the kiln. However, in the upper heat range the intensity of color can become great enough to hide the cones. Dark glasses, a polarizing filter, or blue bottle glass will aid in seeing the cones. Setting the cones in the kiln with no ware behind them will also help. Blowing a steady stream of air into the spy hole will momentarily cool the cones making them visible for a short time. Caution is advised, however, not to get too close to the open hole. The reverse blast of heat or flame coming out after blowing could cause permanent eye damage.

Pyrometers

Pyrometers are available for measuring the actual temperature inside a kiln at a given moment. A pyrometer is a bimetallic thermocouple, protected by a porcelain sleeve, attached to a galvanometer calibrated for temperature. When the thermocouple is heated, electromotive force is generated and the current flow is registered on the meter. Many kilns come equipped with a pyrometer installed. Inexpensive pyrometers can be purchased separately and installed on most kilns. Pyrometers are valuable as indicators of temperature change during all stages of firing and can show when kilns should be speeded up or slowed down. They are also useful in checking the cooling of a kiln, when cones no longer react.

Highly accurate photoelectric optical pyrometers are used to some extent in industry, but their cost is prohibitive for most individuals. Many types of automatic shutoffs, preprogrammed temperature control panels and other mechanical devices are constantly being introduced on the market. For best results, however, the ultimate control is the attentive potter.

Kiln Log

A kiln log in which times and temperatures are noted for each firing is helpful in reproducing successful firings and in noting potential problems before they become disastrous. For instance, if an electric kiln starts to take longer than normal to reach temperature, elements should be changed before they break in mid-firing. If an electric kiln does take considerably longer than usual to gain temperature, it is a good indication that an element has broken. Although an extra long firing might mature many of the glazes, it is best to shut off the kiln, let it cool, and then replace the element. Refiring the kiln to temperature will not harm most glazes.

Fuel kiln logs should note damper settings and air/fuel settings. Because weather conditions affect a firing, these should be noted as well.

Stacking a Kiln

Shelves should be stacked on kiln posts with a three-point support to maintain level and insure greatest stability. Each set of supports should be placed directly over the lower set for rigidity. If a shelf post wobbles, dampen the bottom end and press it into a bit of dry flint and then onto a small pat of fireclay. Set the post firmly on the shelf. After the firing the clay can be easily separated from the shelf and post. It is best to set the posts first and then place the ware accordingly. To make stacking more compact and easier, pieces of similar height should be placed on the same shelf allowing at least one-half inch of space to the underside of the shelf above to afford good heat circulation and leave room for the initial clay expansion. In larger fuel kilns with multiple sets of shelves, a staggered arrangement helps equalize the circulation of heat. To prevent kiln shelves from unduly warping, bisque fire on the uncoated side and glaze fire on the side that has been kiln washed.

A kiln that is well packed will generally fire much more efficiently than one that is loosely stacked.

Bisque Firing

Most studio potters first fire their ware at a low temperature and glaze fire at a higher one. Industry often first fires high then glaze fires low. In either case, this first fire is called the *bisque*, or *biscuit*, fire. Generally, the bisque fire is heated to a temperature between cone 010 and cone 05 (887-1031°C, 1634°-1841°F), depending on the type of clay used. This burns out all the organic materials, drives out the chemically combined water, and irreversibly changes the composition of the clay while still leaving the ware porous enough to

accept glaze. Clay having been fired in this manner can no longer be recycled.

Because of the lower firing temperature and the fact that bisque ware is unglazed, there is no danger of the pots sticking together if they touch during the firing. Therefore, smaller pieces can be placed inside larger ones to save space in the kiln. Objects that are the same size, such as plates or cups, can be set in stacks lip to lip and foot to foot to help prevent warping.

In a fuel kiln, ware should not be placed in a direct line with the flame. The use of *bag walls, muffles,* or *saggars* will help. In an electric kiln, ware should have at least one inch clearance from the elements. Both of these preconditions will prevent rapid, uneven heating of the raw ware which can only invite disaster.

Although some potters prefer to stack a bisque kiln without shelves and fire by eye, for safety and consistent results, shelves and pyrometric cones should be used.

After the kiln has been filled with ware that is bone dry and the cones are properly placed, the firing is ready to begin. Although there are many variations in the way different kilns are fired, a basic bisque firing should start at a low heat for several hours, leaving the door ajar or spy holes open to allow the atmospheric moisture to escape from the ware and from the kiln bricks and shelves as well. Close the kiln and slowly increase the temperature at a rate of about 50 degrees an hour until the water smoking stage has passed. The kiln can then be fired at a rate of 100 degrees an hour by turning switches up at two hour intervals for electrics or increasing fuel/air mixture every few hours until temperature is reached. As an electric kiln nears temperature, it may be necessary to turn one or two switches back from high to equalize the heat throughout. Shut off the kiln, close dampers tight, and allow the kiln to cool slowly. Ideally, cooling the kiln takes twice as long as it took to heat it.

Glaze Kiln

A glaze kiln should be stacked in much the same way as a bisque kiln. Properly washed kiln shelves, three-point shelf support and correctly placed cones must still be used. The major difference is that because the ware has been glazed, no two pieces can touch. There should be at least a finger's width between each piece to prevent them from fusing together and to allow adequate heat or flame circulation throughout the kiln. Pieces should be checked to see that they are properly dry footed. If a piece must be totally glazed, use only high quality refractory stilts for support and be certain that the piece sits securely on the stilt.

The initial stages of the glaze fire can proceed more rapidly than a bisque fire because changes such as water smoking and the burnout of organic materials have already taken place. An advance rate of about 100 degrees an hour is sufficient to increase temperature at a reasonable speed. After red heat, glazes sinter and begin to fuse. As the temperature increases, glazes first cake, and then boil and bubble until they have melted into a smooth glasslike layer. Near the maturing temperature the firing should be slowed somewhat to allow all the volatile materials to escape and the glazes to smooth out. When the cones start to bend, at least a half hour between the maturing of each cone indicates a good rate of firing. After temperature has been reached, the kiln should be cut back just enough to maintain that heat for another one-half hour. This soaking period allows evening of the temperature throughout the kiln and insures complete melting of the glaze. The kiln should then be shut off, damper closed, and cooled very slowly to allow the glazes to stiffen and the clay to contract evenly. Rapid cooling can prevent glazes from smoothing out, leaving pin holes and also dunt, or crack, the clay.

Fast firing is generally not a good idea because it can crack ware, bring about glaze flaws such as crawling or pitting, and cause some glazes to remain underfired. In all cases it should be noted that a slow fire to a somewhat lower temperature will produce equal, if not better, maturing results than a fast fire with its necessarily higher temperature.

Oxidation and Reduction Firing

There are two types of firing which are classified according to the atmospheric conditions inside the kiln; one is *oxidation* and the other is *reduction*. Oxidation occurs when the proper air/fuel mixture is achieved to bring about a bright, clear kiln atmosphere. In the case of electric kilns, because there is no fuel to be burned, the atmosphere is considered to be oxidizing, or more correctly, *neutral*. By increasing the fuel or decreasing the air, a reduction, or smoky, atmosphere can be brought about in a fuel kiln. As an example of these two types of conditions, most campfires start off in reduction and, with luck, go into oxidation.

Both types of firing have their distinct advantages. Oxidation is appreciated primarily for its constancy of effect, brighter colors, its enhancement of under and overglaze effects, as well as its lower firing cost. Reduction brings out subtle color variations in the clay body and glazes as well as accidental effects which impart a sense of the unexpected to the ware.

In earlier times, and to some extent in industry today, blemishes, uneven glaze surfaces and colors, and blacked clay were looked upon as something horrible. Great effort was expended to prevent these "flaws" from occurring. Saddled with only fuel burning kilns, potters developed muffle kilns with completely enclosed refractory chambers, kilns with muffle flues or tubes inside the chamber for the flame to run through, or individual saggars, refractory clay boxes, to protect the ware from being touched by the flame. The advent of the electric kiln made all these practices unnecessary. Today, however, many studio potters and even some industrial firms actively seek the effects flame and smoke produce in clay and glazes and expose the ware to direct flame.

It is virtually impossible to fire reduction in an electric kiln. Some individuals have rigged oil dripping mechanisms or introduce mothballs, wood chips, or oil soaked rags into the firing chamber in an attempt to bring about a reducing atmosphere. These methods sometimes work but they also attack and corrode kiln elements, shortening their life span. The only way to safely bring about certain reduction effects using electricity is by local reduction. Local reduction is not an atmospheric change within the kiln. It is a chemical change in the glaze itself. By introducing small amounts of finely ground reducing agents, such as silicon carbide, into certain glazes, a reasonable facsimile of true reduction can be achieved.

Most often, fuel kilns are used for reduction firings. In the initial heating stages it is more efficient to fire in oxidation, that is, with a clear bright flame and proper air/fuel mixture. It is unwise to begin reduction much below cone 017 (727°C, 1341°F) because this can prevent carbonaceous material from burning out and also cause the ware to bubble or bloat. At cone 017, a reduction atmosphere can be brought about to impart a reduction color effect to the clay body. To change from oxidation to reduction, alter the air/fuel mixture to allow flames to just begin licking out of the spy holes. Close down the damper until some back pressure is also evident through the spy holes. However, closing the damper down too much will choke the kiln and possibly cause a temperature drop. Maintain this light to medium reduction as temperature is increased until the final cone is reached. Heavy reduction during the firing not only wastes fuel but

10-5 Leon F. Moburg
Bottle
Thrown stoneware, fired to
    cone 10 with cone 8
    and 11 decorations
9 x 5 1/2 inches

could cause bloating of the ware and possibly pit or pinhole the glazes. Slow, even firing with medium reduction will bring out the best glaze color and surface.

As the temperature increases, flames will begin to show through the damper or spy holes. At first, there should be a red-yellow tint to it and as the cycle progresses the flame should take on a green to blue hue. If much black smoke is in evidence and the flame is a bright orange, reduction is too heavy and unnecessary. Only a small amount of carbon monoxide is needed to obtain reduction and will acquire all free oxygen present to complete its own combustion, assuring good reduction. The yellow flame contains mostly unburned carbon which plays no part in reduction and is therefore wasteful.

Near the end of the firing cycle, some potters increase the amount of reduction for full saturation of its effects, but heavy smoking often serves only to deposit carbon on the glaze surface making it appear dull and dirty. A long soaking period, wherein the temperature and medium reduction atmosphere are maintained for at least 30 minutes, will better insure full development of reduction glazes. One or two minutes of oxidation, "clearing the kiln," are sometimes employed at the very end of a fire to diminish the possibility of surface scum and to brighten copper reds. The kiln should then be shut off and closed tightly during the cooling period.

Although most potters seem to prefer firing reduction in the higher temperature range from cone 8 to 14, more attention is now being paid to lower temperatures. This is primarily a fuel saving endeavor and also allows for experimentation with new glaze color effects. The use of cones in lower temperature reduction could be a problem because of the iron used in cones below cone 4. Contrary to some statements, cones compounded specifically for this purpose, called Orton Large Iron Free Cones (C/010-C/3), are readily available.

No matter to what temperature or in which atmosphere a kiln has been fired, it should be cooled slowly and not cracked until the temperature is at least 93°C (200°F). This prevents dunting, or cooling cracks from spoiling the ware. The ware should not be removed from the kiln until it can be done with bare hands to prevent the glaze from crazing.

Local Reduction

Because electric kilns rely on electrical resistance to produce heat instead of oxygen, it is not possible to have a true reduction fire without introducing organic materials into the kiln during the latter stages of the firing. When this is done, there is always a certain amount of damage to the kiln elements as well as a risk of possible personal injury. A cleaner, safer way to do local reduction electrically is to mix internal reducing agents directly into the glaze.

The most successful use of the local reduction technique is in the case of copper red glazes. A soda alkaline base glaze works better than a potash base. In either case the glaze should be a fairly fluid one to allow gases to escape during the firing without bubbling the glaze. The amount of copper oxide or copper carbonate needed to induce a red color is surprisingly small, only 0.1 to 0.5 percent addition. The reducing agent most widely used is silicon carbide. It must

10-5

10-6 Engel Kran, 1584
Pitcher
Thrown stoneware, stamped decoration,
 salt glaze
17 inches high
Courtesy: Museum of Fine Arts, Boston
 William Francis Warden Fund

10-7 Thomas Harrington, 1825
Water cooler
Thrown stoneware, salt glaze
20 1/2 inches high
Courtesy: Connecticut Historical Society
Photo: W.F. Miller

10-6

10-7

be finely ground, a mesh of 300 or 400 will give the most even color dispersal. However silicon carbide of 200-mesh or larger can give an interesting speckled effect.

The copper and silicon carbide are added to the glaze in equal amounts along with 1 percent of tin oxide to promote the best color effects. Amounts of silicon carbide above 0.5 percent do not appear to affect the color but can cause excess bubbling and cratering of the glaze.

Boric oxide in a local reduction glaze can promote red, violet, and purple colors, while barium tends to brown out red tones. Colors other than red can be obtained through local reduction by using titanium for shades of blue and small amounts of iron for celadon greens.

Antimony sulfide or molybdenum sulfide can also be used as reducing agents in combination with the same amount of colorant and tin used with silicon carbide, but with varying results.

For best color dispersal, local reduction glazes should be applied more heavily than normal glaze, with more allowance at the foot of a pot for glaze shift.

Because it is not necessary to change the atmosphere inside the kiln, local reduction ware can be put into a regular oxidation firing along with other pieces. It is important, however, that the kiln be fired to the correct glaze maturing temperature and then soaked to allow all the silicon carbide to react. The kiln should then be cooled rapidly to decrease the chances of complete reoxidation which, of course, would cause the reduction colors to disappear.

154

Salt Glazing

The use of traditional salt glazing techniques has been traced back as far as the twelfth century in Germany, when it is purported to have first been used. Basically, salt glazing is a one-fire process wherein the raw ware is stacked loosely in the kiln and brought up close to its maturing temperature. Common salt is then introduced into the kiln and immediately volatilizes, forming a glaze coat on the ware.

Chemically, a series of reactions occur:

$$(1)\quad 2NaCl + 2H_2O \rightarrow 2NaOH + 2HCl\uparrow$$
$$(2)\quad 4NaOH + Q(heat) \rightarrow 2Na_2O + 2H_2O\uparrow$$
$$(3)\quad 2Na_2O + XAl_2O_3 \cdot XSiO_2 \rightarrow 2Na_2O \cdot XAl_2O_3 \cdot XSiO_2$$

At first, the salt reacts with water vapor in the kiln atmosphere and forms sodium hydroxide and hydrochloric acid fumes. Secondly, the heat of the kiln decomposes the sodium hydroxide into sodium oxide and water vapor. The sodium oxide then reacts with the clay surface and forms a sodium alumina silicate glaze. The hydrochloric acid and water vapor mix and exhaust out of the kiln. Herein lies the chief danger in salt glazing. If there is insufficient water vapor to mix with the hydrochloric acid, as is often the case, then deadly chlorine gas is formed. Heavier than air, this yellow brown gas settles in the lungs if inhaled and can cause severe damage and, possibly, death.

It is strongly advised, therefore, that salt glazing be conducted in a very well ventilated area; an outdoor operation is considerably safer.

During the fire, the salt reacts not only with the clay ware, but with everything else, including the shelves, posts, and interior kiln walls. Because this action will be repeated in subsequent firings, it is necessary to have a separate kiln and accompanying furniture set aside for salt glaze only. Best results are obtained in a down-draft type kiln with special ports for introducing the salt.

The walls of the kiln should be coated with aluminum oxide and the kiln furniture coated with a wash of alumina hydrate to slow the inevitable deterioration by the salt. Never use normal kiln wash because it will combine with the salt to become glaze and everything will stick together when fired. Each time the kiln is fired more glaze forms on its interior. It may take a number of firings to *season*, or *ripen*, a kiln, that is, deposit enough soda on the walls to give a good even glaze to all the ware.

The temperature to which the kiln should be fired depends upon the maturing temperature of the clay. Salt glaze can be done on earthenware but seems to give more satisfactory results when fired from cone 4 to cone 10.

The kiln can be heated in oxidation to about cone 017 ($727°C$, $1341°F$) and then given light reduction up to clay maturity to enhance the body color. Near temperature, the damper should be closed more and then scoops or small bags full of wetted salt should be thrown into the kiln. Four to 8 percent of borax added to the damp salt will improve the glaze surface and help prevent crazing. Salting should be done at 10 to 15 minute intervals, three to five or more times to produce adequate glaze coverage. Each time salting is done, the temperature drops. The kiln should be allowed to regain temperature before the next salting. Just how much salt should be introduced into the kiln depends a great deal on the size of the kiln and the desired results. Between 300 to 600 grams of salt per cubic foot of kiln space is suggested as a starting amount on which to base further tests.

Draw trials should be hooked out of the kiln to check glaze coverage between saltings. After the first salting, cones will no longer react properly as heat guides. The use of a pyrometer is recommended. When glazing is considered satisfactory, the kiln should be shut off, closed up, and allowed to cool slowly.

Certain clay bodies react better to salting than others. High silica clays work best. Additions of titanium or magnesia to the body will improve glaze qualities. Iron bearing clays give colors ranging from tan to black depending on the amount of iron available. Other colors can be obtained either by applying engobes or washes to the clay or by adding small amounts of dry color chlorides to the salt mixture before salting.

Because salt vapors do not go down inside pots, interiors must be glazed in the usual manner. Most stoneware glazes work well, but some may be affected in texture or color. Lead glazes are not adversely affected by salting, but should be used with discretion.

Ecology and pollution minded individuals have been experimenting with alternatives to salt glazing. Sodium bicarbonate (baking soda) and sodium carbonate (soda ash) have been used as successful salt substitutes, the by-products of which are carbon dioxide and water, not hydrochloric acid and chlorine gas.

Although the sought after *orange peel* texture of traditional salt glazing is somewhat reduced, it appears that these substances bring out a richer coloration of the clay body and most slip glazes that are used.

10-8 Don Reitz
Ceramic form
Thrown and slab-built stoneware,
    salt glaze
30 inches high

10-8

10-9 Don Reitz
Vase
Thrown stoneware, salt glaze
50 inches high

10-9

10-10 David Halsey
Vase
Thrown stoneware, slip decorated,
    salt glaze
22 x 7 inches

10-10

Raku

Raku gained prominence in Japan as a part of the Zen tea ceremonies of the Toyotomi Shogunate, during the late 1500s. In the 1950s, it became the vogue in western ceramics because it is a method of fast firing clay and near instant gratification. More recently, some potters have begun to approach raku, which means *contentment*, with much greater personal involvement. To achieve this, the potter must really understand the interaction of clay, glaze, and flames because raku has its own process of natural selection. Pieces that are not well thought out or that are poorly made blow up in the kiln.

Working with raku requires an *open* clay body, a small simple kiln, long sturdy tongs, a door hook, asbestos or heavy leather gloves, shatterproof polarized goggles, water containers, and lidded cans filled with leaves or sawdust.

The clay body should be a mixture of coarse-grained clays and organic materials or have from 25 to 40 percent grog in it to withstand the thermal shock of being placed in the intense heat of the kiln and then rapidly cooled. Because the clay must be quite porous and underfired, raku ware is not really suitable for prolonged storage of food or liquids.

The kiln should be fairly small to allow rapid heat buildup between the frequent opening and closing of the door. If the kiln is too large, it will take considerably longer to heat. For the most interesting results, some type of fuel kiln should be used, chiefly because of the initial, or primary, reduction effect that can be induced during the firing, and also because fuel kilns are easy to build or remodel. The kiln should be constructed with a door that is easy to open and close. A spy hole should be well placed for an unobstructed view of the pots while they are being fired. If an electric kiln must be used, it is essential that the current be turned off each time before the door is opened. Because hot air is a good conductor, opening a kiln that is still electrified could be FATAL!

Long sturdy tongs are needed to place the pots into the kiln and remove them after they have reached temperature. A long door hook is used to safely control the hot kiln door. The asbestos gloves protect the hands and goggles are a necessary safety measure for the eyes. The cans for water and combustible materials should be made of metal, not plastic, for safety.

10-11 David MacAllister
Raku bowl
Ash glaze
3 inches high

10-12 Bruce Grimes
The Eternal Tree
Raku slab, incised, stamped
24 x 22 x 8 inches

10-13 Rick Hensley
Raku plate
23 inch diameter

Traditionally, the pot is first pinched into a thick-walled bowl and then carved down to a refined shape. Any method can be used to make a raku form, but certain restrictions should be kept in mind. Corners, constricted shapes, poorly joined pieces, and pots that are too thin or too thick in cross-section all run the risk of cracking or exploding in the kiln. To cut down on kiln losses, the ware should be bisque fired before glazing. It is possible to once fire raku ware, but a superior clay highly resistant to thermal shock must be used and the ware must be completely dried before being placed into the kiln.

Glazes must, of necessity, mature at very low temperatures and have high thermal resistance. Most raku glazes rely on high lead content for adequate fluxing, but good glaze bases can be formulated with frits, colemanite, and other materials. It must be remembered, however, that, because of the fast firing, not all of the chemicals will fully mature and combine. This could lead to toxic illnesses if a raku piece is used extensively for eating or drinking.

Because of the low temperature, usually around cone 022 to cone 08 (585°-945°C, 1085°-1733°F), not only can the usual colorants be used, but others which normally burn out at higher temperatures offer rich effects. Small percentages of tin chloride or silver nitrate will give good luster qualities to pots that undergo secondary reduction. These effects, although exciting, are not as long lasting as true primary reduction inside the kiln because they tend to reoxidize when exposed to air. Small percentages of selenium, cadmium, antimony, and chrome can give bright reds, yellows, and oranges when used alone or in combinations.

While the kiln is being heated, apply glaze thickly to the pots and then thoroughly dry them to get rid of any absorbed moisture. The pieces may be preheated by placing them on top of the kiln.

Wearing gloves and goggles, grasp a pot carefully but firmly with the tongs. Open the door, place the piece in the kiln and quickly close the door. Glazes usually begin to mature, after being put in the kiln, in 3 to 30 minutes depending on kiln size, heat advance, and glaze composition. The best way to tell if a glaze is maturing properly is to look into the kiln through the spy hole. When the glaze has stopped bubbling and has taken on a smooth glossy surface, quickly remove the pot with the tongs. For secondary reduction effects, the pot is immediately placed in a bucket of leaves, sawdust, or grass and covered with additional combustible material. As soon as the heat of the pot ignites the material, cover the bucket and allow the piece to reduce for at least 3 to 5 minutes. This will thoroughly

10-11

10-12

10-13

blacken the clay body, burn in luster effects, and bring out reduction colors. Remove the pot and let it cool naturally. If the immediate secondary reduction effects are to be retained, take the piece from the bucket with the tongs and quench the pot in water. If oxidation color effects are desired, plunge the pot into water right after removing it from the kiln, skipping the combustible material.

Careful observation and good use of the vagaries of the flame, reduction times, and methods can bring to raku a true sense of interaction between pot and potter.

Wet Firing

Wet firing is a technique, unlike raku, by which a freshly made pot can be put into a hot bisque kiln, removed, glazed and fired again, all within a matter of minutes. This technique, developed by Gerry Williams, requires a small two-chamber gas kiln, a special clay body and glazes, all of which are simple to make.

The kiln is the important factor in the success of a wet firing. The basic firing principle appears to be that when a wet pot is closed up in a hot kiln, an envelope of hot wet air immediately surrounds it allowing rapid water removal but preventing explosion. The kiln must therefore have an easily responding draft control.

The kiln is built of K-23 firebrick using silicon carbide shelves as the two floors and roof. The two doors, one for each chamber, must be snug fitting and easily removable. The flame enters through the back of the lower glaze chamber under the floor and goes to the front. It then travels through the chamber to the back of the upper bisque and finally out the top of the front door.

Both stages of firing are conducted simultaneously. The lower glaze chamber maintains a temperature of approximately cone 4 (1168°C, 2134°F) and the upper bisque chamber about cone 010 (887°C, 1629°F). To gauge the temperature accurately a pyrometer should be used.

The clay body is made into a stiff mix from 50 Red Art Earthenware, 50 Jordan Stoneware, 1% barium carbonate, 3% nephylene syenite, and up to 20% fine sand. Add one part by volume of Babcock-Wilcox Bulk Kaowool to one part by volume of the mix, or 1 pound Kaowool to 100 pounds clay. The Kaowool, which is a silica alumina fiber, provides an excellent buffer against thermal shock. Standard stoneware and raku bodies do not work well with this method. However, this body can itself be used for raku.

10-14

Two simple quick melting glazes for wet firing are:

Gloss		Matt	
Frit 3314	81.7	Lithium Carbonate	16.7
China Clay	13.4	Wollastonite	26.1
Tin	4.9	China Clay	23.4
	100.0	Flint	33.8
			100.0

Other glazes which melt between cones 2 to 5 (1142°-1177°C/2088°-2151°F) can be used.

The pots should be fairly small and can be hand built or wheel thrown. Slab pieces often do not survive. Wall sections should be thin and even. Do not allow any drying. Immediately upon completion, use tongs to place the pot into the hot upper chamber of the kiln. The front door is closed while the back flue remains open until the pot is dry. This takes only a few minutes. Then the door is opened slightly and the flue closed. In this way heat flow and humidity are controlled until the pot has dried. Firing then proceeds normally for about one-half hour. The pot is removed, cooled and glazed. Slips or oxide washes can be applied over or under the glaze. The piece is then dried on top of the kiln. When dry it is placed in the hotter lower chamber and fired to temperature in about one-half hour. It can then be removed and, if desired, undergo secondary reduction in a bucket of combustible material.

Firing Defects

The reasons for failure to achieve sought after results in clay work and glazing are many. Even assuming skillful forming techniques, careful handling, and complete drying, defects can still occur when the ware is subjected to the heat of the fire.

Cracks or Exploding in the early stages of firing are caused by rapid water removal. To prevent this, be certain that the ware is well dried in low humidity and the kiln is initially heated very slowly. Making ware with excessively thick walls should also be avoided.

Shrinkage Cracks in tall pieces are caused by the top of the kiln being heated faster than the bottom. This can be prevented by slow heating during the early stages of the firing and careful stacking which helps insure even heat distribution throughout the kiln.

Warping happens when there is a variation in the fired shrinkage or density of the clay. Constructing ware with even wall thicknesses and firing the kiln slowly will prevent the occurrence of warping.

Blebbing, the appearance of raised bumps on the surface of the ware, is caused by air pockets in the clay which swell during the firing. Well kneaded clay and careful construction of forms, leaving no entrapped air, will prevent this flaw.**10-15**

Bloating is similar in appearance to blebbing but occurs, particularly in fuel kilns, when there is insufficient oxygen available in the 350° to 700°C (622°-1292°F) heat range to help remove all carbonaceous material from the clay. Keeping the kiln in an oxidizing atmosphere during this time will bring about complete carbon burn-out.

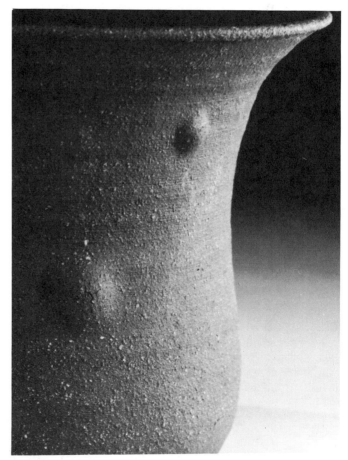

10-15

Black Coring, the blackened center of the clay walls, is caused by reducing high iron-bearing clays too early, which weakens their structure. To prevent this, body reduction should not be started much below cone 017 (727°C, 1341°F).

Dunting, sharp cracks in the clay, occurs during the cooling cycle, around 573°C (1063°F) as quartz inverts, or at 250°-270°C (482°-518°F) when cristobalite inverts. To prevent dunting, cool the kiln slowly and resist the temptation to open it too soon. Occasionally, dunting can occur during the heating cycle. Its characteristic cracks are smooth-edged because the matured glaze has melted into them. These cracks are an indication of a great variation in the thickness of the clay walls from base to upper sections. Ware constructed with even wall thickness will not dunt this way.

A number of defects in fired glazes can be traced to methods of application and firing, but one of the most common problems is closely associated with the interaction of glaze and clay body.

Crazing is the appearance of a network of cracks in a fired glaze. It is primarily a consequence of unequal contraction of clay body and glaze during the cooling cycle wherein the glaze contracts more than the clay. One way to correct this problem is to adjust the expansion properties of the clay body by increasing the amount of silica in the body or by substituting a finer mesh of flint. In clay, the flint remains a crystalline solid and, through its reversible inversion at 573°C (1063°F), can affect the fit of glazes. Since most studio potters work with one clay and many glazes, it is more practical to correct the problem glaze rather than the clay. This is accomplished by reducing the thermal expansion and contraction of the glaze through substitution of oxides which have a lower coefficient of expansion. Crazing may be corrected by one or more changes in the glaze, such as increasing the silica, increasing the alumina, or decreasing the feldspar or other soda or potash materials. Proper heating and cooling cycles will also reduce the possibility of crazing.

Delayed or Moisture Crazing can happen long after the glaze has been fired. Over a period of time a slightly porous clay body can absorb moisture to the extent of causing metakaolin to change to kaolinite. The resulting minute expansion of the clay could cause the glaze to fracture. This can be easily avoided by firing the clay to complete vitrification.

10-16

Shivering is just the opposite of crazing. A glaze which has cooled into excessive compression will split and peel away from the clay body. To remedy this, reduce the amount of silica in the glaze or increase the alkaline oxide content. Equivalent substitution of nepheline syenite for another feldspar can often prevent shivering. Decreasing the flint in the clay body can also help. **10-16**

Fracturing or breaking of the ware usually happens when glaze has been applied thickly to the interior of a piece and thinly or not at all on the outside. When the ware cools, the compression of the glaze causes the clay body, which is in tension, to break at its thinnest point. Increasing the silica content of the glaze and careful glaze application will correct this. **10-17, 10-18**

Crawling, also called *ruckling, beading,* or *curling,* is characterized by areas of ware left bare by the contraction of the fused glaze. In extreme cases, the glaze may roll off the pot onto the kiln shelf. **10-19**

The chief causes of crawling are related to the uneven shrinkage rates between glaze and clay body brought about by using too plastic a clay in the glaze, excessive glaze milling or grinding or high shrinkage glaze constituents, such as zinc or magnesium carbonate. Substitutions of raw materials with less shrinkage, such as calcinated clay or calcined zinc, will help correct this flaw. A tablespoon or two of some type of binder, gum, starch or acrylic medium, will bond the glaze to the clay better and minimize glaze cracks in drying. Too much binder can actually facilitate crawling because of its high rate of shrinkage.

10-17

10-18

10-19

The most common reasons for crawling are related to improper glaze application. Dust and skin oils; overfired bisque; flashed ware that has been unevenly bisqued; thickly applied glaze or a second glaze coating over a completely dry coat; or pots still wet from interior glazing which prevent the outside glaze from adhering well cause the glaze to crawl.

If cracks or tiny holes do appear on the dry surface before firing, light rubbing in a circular motion with a finger will fill glaze powder into the cracks.

Firing ware that is still damp, setting ware too close together for proper ventilation, and rapid heating through the water smoking stage can weaken the glaze layer, as well as its bond to the clay body, and cause crawling.

Peeling occurs when washes, slips or underglazes have been applied too heavily. They act as a dust coat and prevent the glaze from adhering. To avoid this, apply the wash thinly or add binder to the underglaze. **10-20**

10-20

Bubbles are often caused by glaze firing too rapidly. This prevents gases in the clay body and glaze from completely dissipating through the glaze layer. A slower firing near maturing temperature will often cure this fault.

Pinholing is the term for tiny holes which appear in a fired glaze. This may be caused by poor clay preparation, improper glaze application or incorrect firing. Fine grained clay bodies can cause a glaze to pinhole more easily than coarse or grogged clays because the compact density of the clay does not allow easy escape of gases during firing. If the clay body has not been well homogenized before use or if small airspaces remain after kneading, it is possible that the entrapped air could cause bubbles to form under the glaze coat. Underfired bisque ware can absorb glaze too quickly and form tiny air pockets in the glaze. Soluble alkaline sulfate salts in the clay body can form on the surface of the ware and, when dissolved into a glaze, can leave air pockets which, when fired, cause pinholes. Small additions of barium carbonate will render the sulfates insoluble and correct this problem. Soluble salts present in the local water supply can also make a glaze pinhole. These salts can be neutralized by adding a little vinegar to the water.

Glazes which have been stored for long periods begin to decompose and contain gases which can bring about this flaw. Drying the glaze, remixing and screening it will allow these gases to escape. The glaze can then be safely reused.

Ware saturated with water during glazing, violent spray glazing, air trapped between bisque and glaze layers during dipping, overly thick glaze coatings, and a long time interval between glaze coats can all cause pinholing.

Starting body reduction too early can cause carbon deposits to form in the clay. These deposits can become a gas at higher temperatures and cause pinholes in the glaze.

Glazes that are fired to temperature too rapidly or are overfired will often pinhole. Slowing the firing near maturity and soaking the ware for a half hour will allow more time for gases to escape and glazes to flow, healing possible pinholes.

Blistering or Cratering is a more severe form of pinholing wherein bubbles in the glaze burst and leave sharp-edged craters on the surface of the fired glaze. Thick coatings, particularly on the bottom interior of the ware, are apt to blister. Overfiring of a glaze can cause some of its constituents to vaporize and blister. Lead glazes tend to blister if they are subjected to a reduction atmosphere. **10-21**

10-21

Running glazes are those which shift down the sides of the ware and often right off onto the kiln shelf. An application of glaze that is too thick can cause running. Occasionally, the addition of too much colorant to a glaze or overfiring a glaze may cause it to run. To help prevent this, the amount of kaolin in the base should be increased to make the glaze more refractory.

Dull Surface of a glaze is often caused by excessive amounts of insoluble materials in the base, such as tin, rutile, or spinel stains. If the proportion of silica to alumina is too low, or if too much barium or calcium is in a glaze base it will have a dull, rough surface.

The greatest single problem which can bring about many faults in a kiln is inadequate temperature control.

Overfired ware may be under great tension, be too vitreous or have even begun to melt.

Glazes will run, become too shiny, and often be a different color than expected. Seriously flawed, overfired work can rarely be corrected and should be discarded. Occasionally, however, overfiring can bring about pleasing results.

Underfired ware can be too porous, with glazes that are the wrong color, incompletely melted, and have rough pebbly surfaces. Often these problems can be corrected by simply refiring the ware to the proper maturing temperature.

Reapplying glazes to thin areas, filling pinholes or blisters, or applying a different glaze for color and surface effects may be done on flawed ware, which is then refired to the correct maturing temperature. However, because there is no absorption on a glaze-fired surface, reapplication of glaze is somewhat difficult. One way to accomplish this is to slowly heat the ware in a kiln or oven until it is hot. Then, wearing gloves, remove the piece and immediately apply a gum solution over the surface. As soon as the steaming has stopped, apply a thickened coat of glaze, preferably by dipping or spraying. Another method, which is easier to use, is to mix the glaze with acrylic medium and apply it directly without heating. The medium dries to a strong bond, allowing two or three coats of glaze to be applied if needed. In both cases, the work is then fired normally. Low-fired glazes may be applied to high fired ware in the same manner. The ware is

10-22 Jar
18th century Chinese
Thrown porcelain, double crackle glaze
9 x 9 inches
Courtesy: The George Walter Vincent
   Smith Art Museum, Springfield, Mass.

10-23 Vase
18th century Chinese
Thrown stoneware, lava glaze
17 1/2 inches high
Courtesy: The George Walter Vincent
   Smith Art Museum, Springfield, Mass.

then refired to the maturing temperature of the glazes used.

Sometimes, in the case of some glaze faults, the result can be quite pleasing. Controlled crazed glazes, called *crackle* glazes, were sought by Oriental artisans for their cobweb-like effects. Glazes which run, crater, pool or streak can often be attractive on a particular piece. Ultimately, it is up to the clayworker to decide if the foregoing glaze defects are only flaws or have become interesting variations.

10-22

10-23

CHAPTER 11 Kilns, Wheels, and Studio Equipment

11-1 Covered pit kiln
Lejre, Denmark
Photo: Susan Feinsod

11-2 Mud teepee kiln
Lejre, Denmark
Photo: Susan Feinsod

11-1

11-2

Kilns

Over the centuries, many different methods of heating clay to a stage of permanency have been developed, some of which are still in use today. Others have been discarded for their impracticality in modern times, and still others have been recently revived for their educational value, special effects, or just plain enjoyment.

Soon after it was realized that clayware which had been heated in a cooking fire was less apt to break than that which was not, open fire methods were used to harden clay objects. Some African tribes and Indian tribes of the Southwestern United States still use the technique of stacking their ware in a mound which is then covered with combustible material such as dried corn stalks or dung cakes. The material is ignited and allowed to burn down. Because of uneven heating and thermal shock, this method is quite inefficient and losses are often high. Minor improvements in heat efficiency were gained by covering the combustible material with shards of pottery which acted as insulation.

Open pit fires and, later, closed or covered pit fires dug in the ground used the earth to insulate the heat and attain somewhat higher temperatures and longer firing times.

Teepee-like kilns made of sticks tied together in a cone and covered with mud were used during the Iron Age. Replicas of these early kilns are still in use today in the tourist village of Lejre, Denmark.

The first real advance in kiln design and efficiency was probably introduced in the Mediterranean area about five thousand years ago. Kilns were built of dried clay bricks into low circular structures which allowed fuel to be introduced below the ware. No longer were embers relied on to provide heat. Greater amounts of fuel could be introduced to increase the temperature more than had previously been possible.

The type of kiln in which fuel is burned below the ware and allows the heat and gases to exit above is known as an updraft kiln. The Greeks, about twenty-seven hundred years ago, built dome-shaped updraft kilns complete with firebox, ware chamber, and a damper controlled exit stack. The fire could be controlled from a slow heating at the start to a rapid hot flame at the upper temperatures. It could also be adjusted for oxidation or reduction when required for certain color effects.

11-3 Greek updraft kiln

11-4 Chinese *ana-gama*

The art of kiln building was already advanced in the Orient at a time when the Europeans were still using primitive, inefficient methods. The easy access to highly refractory fireclays and kaolins to make into bricks helped the Chinese develop better insulated kilns which retained more heat and reached higher temperatures. Hillside, beehive-shaped kilns, called *ana-gamas*, were the first successful type of kiln to incorporate the downdraft firing system. With the firemouth at one end of the kiln and no chimney in the roof, the heat and flame were forced to travel through the ware to the other end of the kiln before exiting, thus insuring a more even and complete distribution.

The tubular *split bamboo*, climbing kiln as used by the Koreans during the fifteenth century was one long uphill chamber with a few internal partitions. It was an improvement over the *ana-gamas*, but tended to fire erratically.

One of the most effective types of kiln in terms of design was the multichambered hillside kiln developed by the Japanese during the late fifteenth century. A vast improvement over the *split bamboo* kiln, it was constructed as a series of domed chambers connected in a line ascending a hill, making excellent use of the downdraft system. As the fire was built up by stoking wood in the lowest chamber, or firemouth, the flame and gases were forced to pass upward

11-5 Korean split bamboo kiln

167

into the next chamber and then downward into the mouth of the following chamber and so forth before exiting at the stack. When the firemouth reached a high temperature, stoking was begun in the first chamber loaded with ware. After the first chamber reached the desired temperature, stoking continued in the second. Because the fire from one chamber heated the next, less fuel was required for succeeding chambers as the firing continued up the hill. This type of kiln has been in use in China and Japan for centuries and is now experiencing renewed interest among clayworkers in the United States.

Bottle or *cone kilns*, were first constructed in Germany in the early 1700s. Elongated in height and tapering to a narrow opening at the top, these kilns could attain temperatures high enough to mature porcelain. Some of the bottle kilns incorporated a bisque chamber in an upper level. Larger versions of the kiln were called *hovel kilns* because they had an outer bottle-shaped shell for added insulation, as well as weather protection for the firemen stoking the kiln.

All of these kilns used wood for fuel, although, in later times, the Europeans used coal as well. Fuel was cheap, readily available, efficient at high temperature, and helped to create interesting glaze effects caused by falling ash, swirling smoke, and flashing flames. Problems arose, however, if the ware to be fired was to be free of these relatively haphazard effects.

Refractory clay boxes, called *saggars*, were employed to protect the ware from the flames. The drawback to using saggers was that one saggar was necessary to cover each piece or small group of pieces to be fired and, therefore, a great many were needed to stack a kiln. If a saggar broke during a firing (as was often the case), it could destroy many pots at one time.

Eventually, the entire interior of the kiln became one large saggar, better known as a *plate muffle kiln*. The muffle was essentially a house inside the kiln built of refractory fireclay which shielded the ware from the flames encircling the muffle. This type of kiln, and a variation called a *tube muffle* in which the flame goes through refractory tubes, are still in use today.

11-6 Five chamber hillside kiln
Franklin Pierce College,
   Rindge, New Hampshire
Photo: the author

11-7 European bottle kiln

11-8 Section drawings
Left: Plate muffle kiln
Right: Tube muffle kiln

11-9 One car shuttle kiln, model NDS 60
60 cubic foot capacity, gas fired
Courtesy: A.D. Alpine, Inc.

11-10 Modular shuttle kiln
Denver Fire Clay Company
Gas fired
Courtesy: MSI Industries, Inc.

11-11 Roller hearth kiln, model RHK
Gas fired
Courtesy: Ipsen Industries

11-9

11-10

11-11

Because industry needed to be able to fire large amounts of ware at one time, a number of large kiln designs have been developed to facilitate this. A *car kiln* is basically a kiln with a floor on wheels. The car can be conveniently stacked outside the kiln and then rolled on tracks into it for firing. A *shuttle kiln* is a large kiln with a door at each end and two or more moveable cars, one of which can be stacked while the other is being fired. A variation of this is the *envelope kiln* which utilizes two or more stationary cars over which the kiln is rolled, shut, and fired.

All of the kilns mentioned so far are known as *periodic kilns*. That is, they are stacked when cold, heated to temperature, cooled, and then unstacked. The time lost when a kiln is not being fired, therefore, remains an important cost factor. To date, the best solution to this industrial economic problem has been the development of the continuous, or *tunnel kiln.* This long kiln is constantly heated with a series of burners and baffles that keep a low heat near the entrance of the kiln, gradually step up the heat towards the center and maintain cooler temperatures near the exit. The ware is placed on a moving belt, or rollers, and then travels slowly through the kiln. Highly sophisticated versions of this kiln repipe the expended heat over and over throughout the kiln to gain the greatest efficiency.

Today, many versions of both updraft and downdraft kilns are available to schools and studio potters. A few of them are quite good and worth the investment. However, building a comparable kiln can cost considerably less—or more, if not well thought out in advance. Location of the kiln is very important. Prevailing winds, safety factors, local fire, and zoning regulations must be taken into consideration. Should the kiln be fired with natural gas, liquified petroleum, oil, coal, or wood? How big should it be? How many chambers? Should hard or soft firebrick be used? What about house-brick? Commercial castable? Homemade castable? In-sulating blanket? The questions are almost endless.

Currently it appears that studio potters have settled into two basic styles of kiln; one is a *sprung arch* and the other, a *catenary arch* kiln. Both types can be suitably designed for any of the fuels just mentioned, have great size range and can be constructed using any or all of the aforementioned materials. The sprung arch kiln is a box with a curved roof held together by a steel frame. The catenary, on the other hand, is a self-supporting curve arching directly from the floor and requires no additional bracing. The curve is determined by hanging a chain between two nails the floor width apart, forming an arch as long as the kiln is to be high. This is drawn on a template from which a construction form is made.

11-12 Sprung arch kiln
40 cubic foot capacity, gas fired
Courtesy: Gerry Williams
Photo: the author

11-13 Catenary arch kiln
40 cubic foot capacity, gas fired
Courtesy: Roger Harvey
Photo: Felicity Craven

11-14 Catenary construction form
Courtesy: Roger Harvey
Photo: Felicity Craven

11-12

Many sets of plans, pamphlets, and books have been written explaining the processes involved in building a kiln. It would be wise to consult the good ones, as well as individuals who have actually built kilns, before undertaking such a project. The variables are infinite and something which works for one kiln may not work for another.

11-13

11-14

11-15

11-16

11-17

Constructing a Gas Kiln

Recently, many potters have begun to examine the properties of the high temperature insulating blanket and its possible applications to kiln building. The following is a simple, but highly effective, barrel kiln incorporating Carborundum Company's Fiberfrax© blanket, as designed and built by James G. Winegar. These are the materials needed to construct a 10 cubic foot cone 6 portable gas kiln:

50 square feet of 3/4 inch Fiberfrax© Blanket, 9 foot width, 6 pounds/cubic foot density

1/2 gallon F-180 Coating Cement or Sodium Silicate (Water Glass)

One 55 gallon steel drum

One 3 x 3 foot 18 gauge steel sheet

Two 22 inch long 3/8 inch steel rods

Two feet of two inch steel angle iron

Two cans 600°F heat resistant paint

40 1 inch x 1/4 inch carriage bolts and nuts

4 6 inch eyebolts and wing nuts

54 firebricks

The interior and exterior of the 55 gallon drum must first be cleaned of all residue. All paint must be wirebrushed or sandblasted off. The upright barrel is then cut in half, from top to bottom, using a metal cutting blade fitted to an electric saber saw. The barrel is inverted and a 10 inch square draft opening is cut in the center of what is now the top. **11-15,** Two holes 2 inches in diameter are cut in the side of the barrel to serve as spy holes. **11-16,** Two detachable handles are bent from 18 inches of 3/8 inch steel rod with a 4 inch rod welded perpendicularly to each handle for leverage. **11-17,** Two metal straps, 8 inches long, are welded parallel to each other on each side of the barrel into which the handles can be slipped.

After cutting and welding has been completed, the outside of the barrel is sprayed with heat resistant paint.

11-18

11-19

11-20

Later, the Fiberfrax © blanket will be rolled over the edges of the barrel to protect them from heat. **11-18,** To secure the blanket over the edges, metal straps must be cut and bent to conform to the draft hole, bottom, and sides. **11-19,** The four straps for the sides have pieces of angle iron welded to them to later hold the eyebolt closures. **11-20,** Four of the pieces of angle iron are drilled and the other four slotted.

The straps are temporarily clamped to the barrel in their proper positions. Next, 1/4 inch holes are drilled through the straps and the barrel. This is for the bolts needed to later secure the blanket over the edges. In the example shown, forty holes were drilled. Remove the straps after drilling. To protect the bolts from heat, they are put through the holes, threaded end outward, before the Fiberfrax© is placed in the barrel.

After the bolts are placed, the Fiberfrax© is then measured and cut to fit the interior of the barrel. Regular scissors can be used for cutting. Two layers of Fiberfrax© are to be used. **11-21,** The pieces of the first layer are measured and cut to fit exactly to the edges of the barrel. The pieces are then secured to the inside of the barrel using Carborundum Company's F-180 cement or liquid sodium silicate. The cement is brushed on the metal in a thin, even coat. The pieces of Fiberfrax© are laid in place and pressed gently against the barrel. Both barrel halves are lined in the same manner.

11-21

11-22

11-23

11-22, The second layer of Fiberfrax© is cut to size at least 4 inches longer than all the edges of the barrel. This excess will be turned over the edges and strapped down. Cement is evenly applied to completely cover the first layer of Fiberfrax©. The second layer is gently pressed on top. The cement is allowed to set for at least three hours before folding the blanket over the barrel edges. Cement is used to secure the blanket to the outside surfaces. The protruding bolts are pushed through the Fiberfrax© and the straps are placed on and bolted securely. The excess blanket at the draft hole and bottom of the kiln is cut into tabs which are turned over the edges and bolted securely with the straps.

11-23, Eye bolts are put through the holes in the side straps with the threaded end fitting into the slots.

The damper is made of a piece of square sheet metal, 12 x 12 inches. An off-center loop of metal is welded to the top to hold a kiln handle. Two layers of Fiberfrax© are cemented to the underside of the damper and the top is spray painted. The construction of the kiln is now complete.

A firebrick platform is built up of 3 layers of 18 bricks each, forming a 27 inch square. A burner port is made by removing one and a half bricks from the top layer, one brick in from the side. One brick is taken from the middle layer directly below. This forms a burner port with a step in it to push the flame upward into the chamber It is offset to create a spiral flame motion. The extra firebrick can be cut to make two spy hole plugs.

11-24 Frontloading electric kiln
Unique PRO series
3 cubic foot capacity
Courtesy: HED industries, Inc.

11-25 Toploading electric kiln
Model K-18
2.6 cubic foot capacity
Courtesy: L and L
    Manufacturing Company

The kiln is ready to be fired with any type of natural or LP gas burner.

This type of kiln can also be fueled by wood or coal. Instead of a solid platform, a grate is constructed for the kiln to rest on. A four foot tall galvanized stack lined with a single layer of Fiberfrax© and set on top of the damper hole will increase the draft necessary to fire with these materials.

The kiln can be used quite easily for raku firings. If shelves are used, they should be of silicon carbide to withstand the thermal shock stresses of rapid heating and cooling. The glazed ware is stacked and the kiln heated. Because the Fiberfrax© blanket does not exhibit heat color as do firebrick kilns, temperature judgments must be made by relying on the melt of the glazes and color glow of the heating pots. When the raku glazes have fused, the burner can be quickly shut off and one side of the kiln unlatched and easily lifted away. The ware can then be rapidly removed from the kiln for secondary reduction while still red hot. The kiln can be restacked with more ware and fired up to temperature, usually within a half hour.

Electric Kilns

The chief boon to the recent growth of interest in ceramics has been the electric kiln. Unobtrusive, efficient and relatively inexpensive, the electric kiln has brought claywork within the reach of hobbyists, students, and professionals. Although it is possible to build an electric kiln, the proliferation of commercially available styles and sizes at reasonable cost makes entertaining this idea somewhat specious.

Electric kilns are constructed in two types, frontloading and toploading. Frontloading kilns are equipped on one side with a swinging or sliding door for easy reach when stacking. The main drawbacks to frontloading kilns are the awkward way that kiln shelves have to be guided into the kiln, the considerable cost involved for just the door bracing, and the gross weight of the kiln itself. Toploading kilns are generally less expensive because many of them are made up of removable ring sections and require no special bracing for the door on top. Drawbacks are the rapid cooling in comparison to the more heavily insulated frontloading kilns, the occasional problem of unnoticed bits of kilnwash or kiln shelf falling on the ware below, and pots slightly too tall being unknowingly damaged as a shelf is being set. An electric kiln is fired with metal elements placed in grooves in the chamber walls. These elements resist live electric current and in so doing, generate heat.

11-24

11-25

175

Three types of element wiring are available for electric kilns. For low temperatures, below cone 06 (991°C, 1816°F), Nichrome wires can be used. These are less expensive than Kanthal A wire, necessary for work up to cone 5 (1177°C, 2151°F). The more expensive Kanthal A-1 wire elements are required for temperatures up to cone 10 (1285°C, 2345°F). Much higher temperatures can be attained by using silicon carbide rods as the heating elements. Because a transformer is necessary to operate them, the cost is prohibitive for the individual potter. The variations in cost between earthenware temperature kilns and those designed for stoneware are because of the different types of electric element and refractory bricks required for each.

For greater diversity and flexibility of firing temperatures, a higher temperature kiln, in the long run, will be more than worth the added initial expense. Kiln size is also important. Again, over a period of time, a larger kiln will more than pay for itself.

Although there is no danger of fire or blowout as with fuel kilns, for safety, an electric kiln should be at least 12 inches from any walls or other equipment and on a level cement or concrete floor. If the floor is wood, it should be covered with a sheet of transite or asbestos. The kiln can be placed on cement blocks for greater air circulation underneath.

Adequate ventilation is necessary to prevent the studio from filling with escaping gases from the clay and glazes during firing.

It is very important that sufficient electric power be available to service the kiln. Be sure to have the correct line requirements for the kiln size. Often it is wisest to install a separate line and fuse system specifically for the kiln rather than to rely on existing lines within the building. A separate meter is not necessary but would be advisable in a school or commercial operation to evaluate cost. A simple way to estimate the cost of firing a kiln is to multiply the kilowatt rating by the local unit cost of electricity and then multiply this by the firing time.

Solar Kilns

The latest movement in the growth of kiln design has been the few tentative steps taken by some toward developing a practical solar kiln.

An apparatus which could be loosely called a solar kiln was developed by Ehrenfried Walter Tschernhausen around 1690. The furnace consisted of large "burning glasses," or lenses, which focused the rays of the sun onto a small refractory box, heating it and its contents to high temperatures. In collaboration with Tchernhausen, Johann Friedrisch Bottger attempted to melt various substances into gold. Although they never achieved this goal, they were able to develop Germany's first high temperature true white porcelain.

The recent solar kiln experiments have used large Mylar disc reflectors, mirrors, or magnifying glasses to focus the sun's rays at the fire box. To date firebox size has been severely limited because of the relative size of the reflectors needed to concentrate enough sunlight to promote sufficient heat.

11-26

11-27

Wheels

It is said that Athene, the goddess of ceramics, invented the potter's wheel and used it to make vases. The ancient Egyptians ascribed to the god Khnum the first use of the potter's wheel with which he fashioned the world-egg. In either case, it can be assumed from excavated vessels that some type of wheel was actually in use in Mesopotamia around six thousand years ago. The wheel was most probably a smooth stone which rested on another and was turned by hand. In Mexico a similar type of wheel, consisting of two clay plates, is still used by many village potters.

The first true momentum wheel was probably developed in early China. It was made of a large stone centered on a smaller pivot stone. At the top edge of the large stone a stick was inserted into a hole and was used as a crank to spin the wheel. Potters in Nepal and other countries still use this wheel today.

Other types of wheels have been used over the centuries, some spun by one person while another did the throwing and still others powered by wind or water. Many European potters still favor the old-style treadle, or side-kick, wheel rotated by a foot operated swing arm.

The potter's wheel which offers the best mechanical advantage is a sit-down kick wheel. The wheel head is connected by a shaft through bearings to a balanced flywheel below. Clay is placed on the wheel head and the flywheel is then kicked up to speed. If the flywheel is heavy enough, 100 to 150 pounds or more, its momentum will continue long enough for a pot to be finished. If the wheel slows down, a few light kicks will easily bring it up to speed.

About as many different designs for wheels have been developed as there are potters. Plans, parts, kits and complete wheels of wood or metal are all commercially available. No matter what style of wheel is preferred, the primary concerns should be comfort, adequate flywheel weight, and smoothness of operation. A homemade wheel built with an automobile driveshaft and using a concrete filled tire as a flywheel can cost one-tenth as much as a commercial wheel and operate as efficently

For added convenience, most kickwheels can be modified to operate with a friction drive motor.

Electric wheels also come in many different styles, the best of which are those with variable speed control. Gear drive motors provide the best response. However, they are also the most expensive. Any other drive mechanism, such as a rubber cone or belt type, should be tested for limited slip and must have positive adjustment capability. Anything less should not be considered.

11-28 Wooden kick wheel, model KW
Courtesy: Robert Brent Company

11-29 Steel frame kick wheel, model J
Courtesy: Robert Brent Company

11-30 Electric potter's wheel, model RK-2
Shimpo Industries Company, Ltd.

11-28

11-29

11-30

Studio Equipment

Along with a good kiln and wheel, other equipment is necessary for efficient operation. Some type of wedging surface is needed to properly prepare clay for use. It could be a large block of smooth plaster, a piece of unpolished marble, asbestos board, or a canvas covered plaster wedging table.

A good quality gram scale is needed to weigh glaze batches accurately. A household scale is useful for weighing clay or plaster.

A laboratory test sieve of 50- to 80-mesh is good for screening glaze or clay slip. A kitchen strainer can be used to sift coarse materials like grog.

Some glaze materials may need to be ground more finely before they can be used. A porcelain mortar and pestle can do the job well for small amounts. If a lot of grinding is to be done, a relatively expensive ball milling apparatus may be needed.

An aluminum or cast iron bench wheel is helpful when hand building or decorating. Plastic "lazy-susans" are not very reliable.

Inexpensive plastic buckets in different sizes are handy to store clay, slake clay scraps, hold water, and mix glazes. Airtight plastic containers are good for storage of glaze materials. Heavy plastic bags are useful for storing clay; lightweight bags protect ware from drying out too soon.

A studio can almost never have enough shelving. Glaze materials must be kept in easy reach; a place is needed to keep wet pots; damp pieces require room to dry; bisqueware requires a place to await glazing; and finished work must be stored as well.

Along with throwing tools, there can never be too many trimming tools or brushes. A carpenter's angle, a level, calipers, putty knives, heat lamp, funnels, sponges, syringes, paddles, a rolling pin, guide sticks, plaster bats or boards to place ware on, paper and cloth towels are a few items that can make a studio function smoothly.

An important point to remember is that clay, glaze, and plaster can rapidly clog plumbing. If some type of easily emptied sink trap is not installed, a bucket should be at hand to prewash everything before using the sink. Periodically, the bucket should be drained and its contents disposed of. If separate buckets are used, uncontaminated clay can be recycled.

CHAPTER 12 Plaster

Plaster can be used to make bats for drying clay and bats for the wheel, as well as molds for making multiples of an object. Plaster is pulverized calcined gypsum, manufactured in many grades of hardness. In the ceramic studio, Regular Pottery Plaster or Number One Pottery Plaster are the best to use because of their hardness and porosity. Plaster is most economical when purchased in 100 lb. bags. It should be stored, airtight, in a warm dry place to prevent moisture from being absorbed.

For best results plaster should always be added to water by weight. The consistency ratio of Regular Pottery Plaster is 72; Number One Potter Plaster, 66. This means that 72 pounds of water must be added to 100 pounds of Regular plaster and 66 pounds of water to Number One plaster for the correct mix. For smaller projects, it may be easier to figure a ratio of 1 quart of water to 2.75 pounds Regular plaster or 3 pounds Number One plaster.

How To Make a Drying Bat

A wooden form is set up on a smooth surfaced table or board and secured with clamps. Clay is pressed around the outside edges of the mold to prevent the plaster from leaking out. The volume of the mold is measured. **12-1,** In the example, the mold is 14 x 19 1/2 x 1 3/4 inches. Multiply these numbers together to derive the cubic measurement. 14 x 19.5 x 1.75 = 477.75 cubic inches. This number is divided by 81, the approximate volume of a quart of Number One plaster, to find the number of quarts needed: 477.75 ÷ 81 = 5.89 qts. For a margin of safety, round the total to six quarts. Multiply this figure by 3.0 to get the weight of dry plaster: 6 x 3.0 = 18 pounds.

12-2, Mold separator or tincture of green soap is applied to all surfaces that the plaster will touch. **12-3,** For reinforcement, chicken wire is placed in the mold. Sift the 18 pounds

12-1

12-2

12-3

179

12-4

12-5

of plaster into the 6 quarts of room temperature water and allow it to slake for 5 minutes. Stir gently from the bottom to mix the plaster and get out air bubbles. The best test for consistency is to draw a finger over the surface of the plaster. **12-4,** When the mark remains momentarily, pour the plaster gently but quickly into the mold. Jar the table or board a few times to force all the air bubbles to the surface and blow lightly on them to break them.

Allow the plaster to set. As the plaster sets, it crystallizes, giving off heat. **12-5,** When the plaster is cool, it is safe to remove the mold. The bat should be allowed to dry in a warm place for a few days before it is used.

A plaster bat for the wheel is made in the same way as a drying bat. A pie tin, pizza tin, or a commercial bat ring can be used to make different diameter bats. When making a drying bat, it is always a good idea to have a few pie tins ready to take any extra plaster mix. In any event, the bat ring should be measured, the mix calculated, and the plaster poured. After the plaster has set, a few light taps on the back of the tin will release the bat.

Making Plaster Molds

Many methods of mold making require plaster lathes or template equipment to develop models. The following methods are simple and direct. They also allow more freedom to design an object for reproduction which does not have to be completely symmetrical.

One-Piece Press Molds

A one-piece press mold is an easy way to make a limited number of multiples of a tile, relief or other simple object. The object to be reproduced is fashioned from a solid block of clay. It is important that there be no undercuts in the design. Otherwise, the object will not come away easily from the mold.

After the model is completed, place a wooden form around it with at least one inch clearance everywhere, including the top. **12-6,** Secure the form and put clay around the seams. Apply green soap over all the surfaces. Calculate the volume of the mold to find the amount of plaster mix needed. Estimate the volume of the model and subtract this amount from the total. Or, better still, have enough pie tins available to take the excess plaster. Mix the plaster and pour it. **12-7,** After the plaster has set, the model may be pulled out and the mold allowed to dry for a few days.

12-6

12-7

12-8

12-9

12-8, When the mold has dried, press clay into it. Force the clay into all parts of the mold, maintaining an even thickness throughout. After the mold has been filled, allow the clay to stiffen. Turn the mold onto some slats and allow the clay to continue drying. If there are no undercuts, the clay object will simply drop out of the mold after having shrunk sufficiently.

12-9 Author
Moses
Press molded stoneware, walnut
24 x 14 inches
Courtesy: B'nai B'rith Members'
 Insurance Program
Photo: the author

12-10 Penny Caroline Hood
Liz
Press molded porcelain, salt glaze
13 x 12 inches

12-10

12-11

12-12

Two-Piece Molds

Draw a line down the center of the model to be cast and place it on its side. **12-11,** Build clay around the lower half of the model up to the center line and at least one inch away from all sides. **12-12,** A flexible form is then secured around the model and the clay. Soap all surfaces. Calculate the volume of the mold, mix and pour the plaster. After the plaster has set, turn the model over and remove the clay. **12-13,** Cut at least three keys into the plaster mold to later position the halves. Secure the form around the model and half mold. Soap all surfaces well. Mix the second batch of plaster and

12-13

12-14

pour. **12-14,** After the plaster has cooled, remove the form, separate the two halves of the mold, and take out the model. Allow the mold to dry completely before using. In the example, each half was pressed with clay. The halves were tied together and the clay smoothly joined. When the clay had stiffened, the mold was removed and the basic form altered to create a series of different heads.

A similar mold for slip casting should have a *gate*, or opening, in which to pour the slip. If it is a two-piece mold, tie it together and set it with the gate at the top. Fill the mold with slip and let it stand until the slip wall has built up to the desired thickness. Pour out the excess slip and let the mold drain upside down. After the clay has stiffened, the mold may be opened and the piece allowed to dry. Parts of one casting may be joined with parts of others while they are still leather hard.

12-15

12-16

12-17

12-18 *I-Ching* Vase
18th century Chinese
Press molded porcelain
10 1/2 x 5 inches
Courtesy: The George Walter Vincent
  Smith Art Museum, Springfield, Mass.

12-19 Richard Shaw
S on a Pillow
Slip cast porcelain
8 1/2 x 7 x 5 inches
Courtesy: Quay Gallery

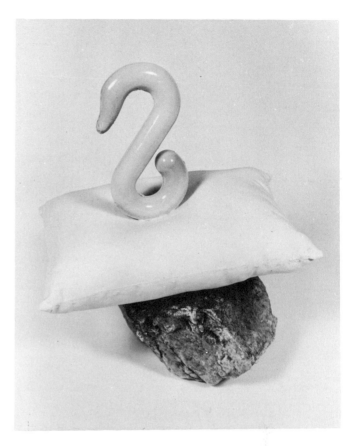

CHAPTER 13 Marketing

Marketing ceramics is as complex as marketing in any other field. The following are notes on some basic aspects of marketing practices.

First it is necessary to decide what type of work is to be produced. Is it to be easily manufactured utilitarian ware, reasonably priced for rapid turnover? Will it be ware that is still utilitarian but individualized by special finishing effects and glazes which therefore demand a higher price? Or is it to be one-of-a-kind nonutilitarian objects which take longer to construct, are higher priced, and therefore appeal to a highly selective market?

Along with this decision, it is necessary to research the locale to discover whether the particular type of work is readily marketable. The artistic consciousness and monetary status of the community can play a large part in the successful marketing of a particular type of clay work. Handsomely fashioned candleholders might be snapped up by collectors in one area and yet remain on the shelves indefinitely in another. The same holds true for price. In some localities a style of casserole might sell for 35 or 40 dollars, whereas the same type in another place might bring less than 30 dollars.

The next step is to decide what type of sales outlet should be used. Should ware be sold directly from the studio, at a quality craft shop, in a department store, or through an exclusive gallery? Museums, craft associations, and other organizations often have well established sales outlets which take a small percentage of the sale price. They can be a valuable source of income but usually at a lower volume than a commercial establishment.

Although it may be possible to realize a greater profit by selling work directly from the studio, some important factors ought to be considered. Dealing directly with the public takes time away from production. During the half hour spent in conversation while selling a 10 dollar pot, a half dozen 20 dollar pots could be made. The added bookkeeping, selling, care of the display area, packing, shipping, and other duties of a retail sales operation might necessitate the hiring of additional help.

When dealing with retail outlets, work should be sold outright. Consignment selling can be a big headache. Virtually no other manufactured commodity is sold in this way. Somehow craftspeople have allowed themselves to become the financial benefactors of a great number of dealers. While it is true that a craftperson's percentage on the sale of consigned work may be higher than on work sold outright, 66 percent of nothing is much less than 50 percent of something. Suppose four different dealers each have 500 dollars worth of work in their stores for a period of three months and sell nothing. That amounts to 2000 dollars which has, in effect, been in limbo. It has not even earned the interest a bank gives for holding the same cash amount for that period of time. Further, it has cost the dealers nothing, and has given them no real motivation to push the work. On the other hand, had they purchased outright, the dealers would be much more strongly motivated to sell the wares in order to recoup their investment, and the craftsperson would have 1000 dollars to live on or put into further production.

Aside from not knowing which works are selling, months might pass before a craftperson receives payment for works that have been sold. In the event of loss or damage of a consigned work, a question can arise as to whose insurance covers the article, the craftperson's or the dealer's. There are other potential legal problems related to consignment. Suppose a dealer goes bankrupt or dies. All the creditors and heirs can rightfully assume that everything in the shop is owned by the dealer and is therefore part of the estate. Unless there are specific contracts to the contrary, the craftperson may be hard put to prove ownership of consigned items.

The only time a consignment agreement might be worthwhile is with an object that is large, experimental, or very expensive. In this case, while both dealer and craftperson could benefit from the exposure of the work, the dealer might not be in a position to buy. If the dealer is reputable and has purchased outright from the craftperson before, a special limited consignment arrangement could be written. This might state that the work would be shown for a period of, perhaps, 90 days with the dealer assuming full responsibility. If the object has not been sold by that time, the craftperson should remove the work, exchange it for another, or in some way end the particular agreement.

Under any other circumstances work should be sold outright. The usual dealer's share is 50 percent of the list price. While this might at first seem high, when overhead, advertising and other requirements of operating a retail establishment are taken into consideration, the amount is not unreasonable.

Discounts should be avoided in most cases. If discounts are offered to friends or prices are lower in the studio than in a retail outlet elsewhere, problems can arise. If a dealer discovers that a craftperson is underselling to any extent, it is fairly certain that the dealer will not reorder from that individual. If the public finds out that some buyers are getting discounts, they will all rightfully expect similar treatment. Although discounts may guarantee immediate capital, over the long run the practice can harm a craftperson's reputation for integrity.

The only discounts that should be considered are the legitimate wholesale discounts for dealers, usually 50 percent; a trade discount for architects and designers, usually 30 to 40 percent; and a 1 or 2 percent discount on merchandise payments received within ten days of billing. An individual who purchases a large number of works at one time totalling more than an amount predetermined by the craftperson may be entitled to a discount of up to 10 percent. Any other discounts may actually be illegal according to the Robinson-Patman Act, Federal legislation designed to prevent unfair price discrimination.

At this point a few words need to be said about the craft fair. Taken at face value, it can be a great advantage to many people. The craftperson can set up a display, have a happy few days, make some quick money, and go home. However, more often than not, the craftperson is the one who benefits least. A fair is usually run primarily as a money making proposition for its operators. The general public often regards a fair as a vast sideshow and bargain hunting event. This attitude is unfortunately perpetuated by some craftpeople who lower their prices or bring second rate work for quick sale. An individual who offers high quality work and demands a fair price often does not sell well. Good work shown alongside inferior work tends to look as poor.

Can a profit really be made at a craft fair? The time spent packing, traveling to the fair, unpacking, setting up a display, repacking, and returning to the studio should be taken into account. If the money generated by sales at the fair favorably offsets the lost production time, then showing at a fair should receive active consideration.

This is not to say that all craft fairs are bad. Many have earned well deserved reputations for quality and have been in successful operation for years. A few facts should be ascertained before undertaking the venture: previous average sales; volume of traffic; how it is financed, whether by admission fees, entry fees or percentage of sales; how well it is advertised; and if it is for professionals or hobbyists can help decide if it is worthwhile to enter.

A number of different factors should be taken into consideration when establishing the list price of an object. It is essential, therefore, that accurate records be kept of all expenses. First, the cost of operating a studio should be determined. Find out what the yearly costs are for electricity, heat, telephone, rent, insurance, and taxes. Determine the total cost of all materials and how much it costs to fire the kiln.

A personal living wage must be established. Wages for any assistants and the salary or commission of any salespeople or agents must also be included. Decide how much to pay someone who works on a wheel. If it is 5 or 10 dollars an hour, this should be figured into the studio operating cost.

The time that it takes to make an object—to trim, dry, bisque fire, glaze and glaze fire—must be taken into account as well.

Inventory, handling, packing, shipping, equipment depreciation, advertising and promotion must also be included in production costs.

Add all of these figures together to arrive at the total operating cost for a year. Break this down into an hourly production rate. Determine the time it takes to produce a certain object and multiply this by the hourly production figure to derive the actual cost of production.

At this point the figure shows only the expense encountered to make an item with no profit margin. A reasonable profit for hand produced work is 100 percent of the production cost. This is added to the production cost to get the wholesale cost of an item. The list price, or fair market price, is twice the wholesale price.

The price of most claywork can be figured in this way. However, artistic merit should not be disregarded. If a work has an exceptionally fine glaze, or if the form has a unique appearance, more money can be included in the list price. One-of-a-kind objects often demand higher prices. The reputation of the craftperson can also warrant increased prices.

Competitive prices are also a determining factor in the list price of an object. In a certain area, if a six-inch hanging planter will sell within a 10 to 20 dollar price range, a similar planter priced at 40 dollars probably will not sell.

Even with all of this accounting, a periodic review and revision of prices should occur. The price of work offered for sale should be adjusted to reflect any increase in the cost of materials and production expenses as well as any national cost of living changes. Increased demand for a craftperson's work is also a legitimate call for an increase in prices.

A great deal of confusion can be dispelled if the price shown on the tag of an object is stated as its list price. It then is a simple matter for legitimate buyers to multiply this by their appropriate wholesale, trade, or special discount to find their wholesale price. The general public also knows immediately how much the item will cost.

Fearful of lack of sales, many newcomers to the craft market, and even some experienced craftpeople, tend to underprice their ware. Not only can this reduce profit, but it may actually inhibit sales. Seeing a vase priced less than might be anticipated, a knowledgeable collector might wonder if the work is made of inferior materials, if there are hidden cracks, or if it is a copy. An impression of poor quality is immediately conveyed.

Once a price has been set, do not modify it under pressure. Too many craftpeople waver, and they lower prices on demand from potential buyers. Be polite, but be firm. Hedging on a price will only spur demand for lower prices on all items in stock, and shortly the entire operation can become a losing proposition. There is no need to be embarrassed by holding to the price a piece deserves, nor

any reason why craftspeople should have less pride in their product than any other manufacturers. If a particular technique is used, it should be pointed out. The buyer should be made to understand that the handcrafted work has individual qualities which make it special.

Try not to take criticism personally. It can be very difficult to have someone turn down an object who is divorced from the time, effort, and loving care involved in its creation. If selling is important, however, distance must be maintained between the object and the craftperson. If well designed and executed, a work will stand on its own merit and a craftperson can ask and receive a fair market price.

Dictionary of Ceramic Terms

absorption   The capacity of a material to soak up liquid.

acid   One of three types of compound that constitute a glaze, the other two being basic and neutral, or amphoteric. The acid group is symbolized by the radical RO_2.

adsorption   The collecting of liquid on a surface by condensation.

aeolian   Wind blown.

agate ware   Ceramic objects made to resemble marble by combining layers of different colored clays.

air-floated   Refers to powders whose particles have been separated by weight by exposure to a stream of air.

alkalies   Base compounds of sodium, potassium and the alkaline earths. Functioning as fluxes, they combine with and lower the fusion point of silica at relatively low temperatures.

amorphous   Without specific form. In chemistry, having no crystalline structure.

amphoteric   Chemically neutral. Can function as an acid or a base.

armature   A framework around which clay can be modeled.

baffle   A wall or barrier made of refractory materials which directs the flow of heat and flame in a fuel kiln.

bag wall   See *baffle*.

ball mill   A jar filled with carborundum chips which, when rotated, will blend or grind glaze or clay body ingredients.

banding   A method of applying a glaze or slip decoration by holding a brush tip against a rotating pot.

banding wheel   See *bench wheel*.

basalt ware or **basaltes**   Black, unglazed stoneware developed in 1772 by the Wedgewood potteries in England.

bas-relief   Raised or indented patterns which remain close to the surface plane.

bat   A disk or slab of plaster or other material used for drying clay or supporting clay forms while being worked.

batch   The ingredients of a glaze formula weighed in correct proportions for a specific blend.

bench wheel   A portable turntable for rotating pottery being formed, decorated or otherwise worked.

binder   A substance used prior to firing to increase glaze adherence or greenware strength.

bisque or **bisquit**   Clay which has been fired once, unglazed.

bisque fire   First firing of a clay to drive out chemically combined water and carbonaceous materials prior to glazing.

bitstone   Coarse silica sand used in saggars to support thin porcelain ware during firing.

blistering   Air bubbles appearing in a glaze after fast firing.

blowhole   An opening at or near the top of a kiln which facilitates steam escape or cooling.

blowout   The explosion of clay in the kiln caused by the sudden escape of steam resulting from rapid heating or the presence of impurities.

blunge   To mix clay or glaze with water to form a liquid suspension.

blunger   A machine with rotating arms used to mix large quantities of clay slip or glaze.

bone china   A creamy, transparent, English soft porcelain fluxed with ash from animal bone.

bone dry   The condition of unfired clay that has no absorbed moisture other than natural humidity.

bottle kiln   An updraft kiln in the shape of a tapering bottle, commonly found in Europe.

b.t.u.   British thermal unit. The amount of heat needed to raise one pound of water one degree Fahrenheit.

burnish   Using a smooth object to polish the surface of leather-hard clay.

calcine   To heat to the temperature necessary to drive off the chemically combined water, carbon dioxide and other volatile gases.

calorie   Metric unit of heat. The amount of heat necessary to raise one gram of water one degree centigrade.

carving   Decorating by cutting into the clay surface.

castable   A mixture of sand, cement and refractory materials used to make kiln walls and kiln furniture.

casting or **slip casting**   A process of forming a clay object by pouring clay slip into a hollow plaster mold.

catalyst   A substance which causes or accelerates chemical change.

celadon   The French name for jade-like green colors derived from iron bearing reduction glazes.

china   Whiteware clay bodies glazed at a lower temperature than that at which they are bisqued.

china clay   See *kaolin*. A white firing, highly refractory primary clay.

chün glaze   A milky blue, opalescent, high temperature reduction glaze developed in fourteenth century China.

coefficient of expansion   The percentage of change in length or volume per unit of change in temperature of a material.

coil   Rope-like roll of clay used in hand building.

collaring or **necking**   A method of narrowing the neck of a pot by squeezing in with the fingers as the pot revolves on the potter's wheel.

colloid   A gelatinous, homogenous substance.

combing or **feathering**   Decorating by gently drawing a coarse comb or feathertip through contrasting rows of wet clay slip or glaze.

cone or **pyrometric cone** A small triangular pyramid made of ceramic materials that are compounded to bend and melt at specific temperatures. The cone serves as a time-temperature indicator of heat work in a kiln.

crackle glaze A glaze developing minute cracks which are considered decorative and are often accentuated by rubbed-in coloring material.

crawling Separating of the glaze coat during firing, exposing areas of unglazed clay.

crazing The undesirable formation of a network of cracks in the glaze caused by uneven clay or glaze contraction.

damp box A cabinet in which unfinished clay objects are stored to retard their drying.

damper A device used to adjust the draft in a fuel kiln by opening or closing the flue.

de-air To remove air from clay.

deflocculant A substance used to bring about better suspension of a material in a liquid by neutralizing the electronic charge of its particles.

deflocculate To evenly disperse particles throughout a liquid.

delft ware Earthenware clay objects coated with a lead-tin glaze which usually have a blue overglaze decoration. Developed in Holland during the seventeenth century in imitation of Chinese procelain.

della robbia ware Ceramic sculpture or relief plaques of glazed terra cotta, produced in Florence by the family of Lucca della Robbia during the fifteenth century.

devitrification The loss of gloss due to recrystallization of a glaze upon cooling.

dipping Coating pottery by immersing it in slip or glaze.

dissociation point The temperature at which a substance decomposes into its constituent parts.

draw trial A sample taken from the kiln as it is being fired to gauge the progress of the firing.

dry foot The bottom of a pot which has been cleaned of all glaze before firing.

dunting Cracking of fired ware in a kiln which has cooled too rapidly.

earthenware Clay that matures at a low temperature but remains porous.

effervesce To give off gas bubbles.

efflorescence Dry or crystallized white scum occuring on the surface of fired ware caused by unneutralized soluble salts.

eggshell porcelain Porcelain with walls so thin that it is translucent.

egyptian paste Low-fire self-glazing porous clay developed in ancient Egypt.

electrolyte A deflocculating agent. An electrical conductor which dissociates into ions in a suitable medium.

elements High resistance wire coils or bars used as the heat source in an electric kiln.

emboss To decorate a surface with raised ornamentation.

empirical formula See *molecular formula.*

engobe A slurry of glaze materials used as decoration on green or bisque ware.

equivalent weight See *mole.*

eutectic The lowest melting point of a mixture of materials, usually below the melting points of the individual materials.

extrusion The process of making shapes by forcing clay through a die.

faïence The French term for tin-glazed earthenware first made at Faenza, Italy, during the fifteenth century, in imitation of Spanish majolica.

fat clay A very plastic clay.

feathering See *combing.*

feldspar A common mineral found in most igneous rocks from which some clay and glaze materials are derived.

fettle or **fettling** To finish or smooth the surface of leather-hard clay. Also to trim the excess clay from cast ware.

filler A material with little or no plasticity used to promote drying and reduce shrinkage of clay bodies or engobes.

filter press A machine which removes the excess water from clay slip by pressure to make it into plastic clay.

firebox A combustion chamber of a gas, oil or wood-fired kiln directly below or beside the ware chamber.

firebrick A refractory insulation brick.

fireclay A clay used in clay bodies for its heat-resistant quality. Also used in the manufacture of kilns and other refractory equipment.

firing The heating of clay or glaze to a specific temperature.

fit The correct adjustment of a glaze to a clay body.

flaking The peeling off of a glaze or slip from a clay surface.

flashing Flame touching a pot in the kiln or the resultant color change of clay or glaze.

flocculate To cause the aggregation of clay particles.

flocs Thin, plate-like, oval crystals of a clay molecule.

flue The space around the ware chamber of a kiln through which heating gases pass from the firebox to the chimney.

flux A substance which promotes the melting of silica in a glaze.

foot The base of a ceramic piece.

frit A mixture of glaze materials that is melted and then reground to eliminate toxic effects or solubility of the raw materials.

fusion point The temperature at which a clay or glaze material melts.

glaze A glass-like coating fusion bonded to a ceramic surface by heat.

glaze fire A cycle during which glaze materials are heated sufficiently to melt and form a glassy surface coating when cooled.

glost fire Another term for glaze fire.

greenware Unfired clay objects.

grés French term for stoneware.

grog Fired clay that has been crushed into granules which may be added to a clay body to increase strength, control drying and reduce shrinkage.

grout Mortar or similar compounds used to consolidate objects by filling spaces between them.

gum A natural gum, such as gum arabic or gum tragacanth, which is used as a binder in glaze to promote better adherence to clay.

hakeme Japanese for "brush grain." A decorating technique of applying an engobe with a stiff broom-like brush.

hard paste A hard, white, translucent clay body fired to cone 12 or above; a true porcelain.

hare's fur See *temmoku*.

high relief A strongly raised or deeply carved pattern.

igneous Produced under conditions which involve intense heat.

impressing Method of decorating by stamping into a clay surface.

incising Engraving a decoration into unfired clay.

ironstone china A term for certain mid-temperature soft paste porcelains manufactured in the United States during the eighteenth and early nineteenth centuries.

jiggering An industrial method of forming a pot on a revolving mold which shapes the inside while a template makes the outside contour.

jollying The reverse system of jiggering. A method of forming a pot between a revolving mold which shapes the outside and a template which shapes the inside.

kanthal A high resistance metal alloy used in the manufacture of heating elements for electric kilns.

kaolin See *china clay*. The anglicized form of the Chinese term for clay. Kao-Lin, meaning "high hill," probably refers to Kaoling, the mountain in China where this white clay was first discovered.

kaolinize The natural conversion by weathering of feldspar into clay.

kiln A furnace for calcining or firing ceramic products.

kiln furniture Refractory shelves, posts and other equipment placed in a kiln to hold ware during firing.

kiln wash A refractory mixture, usually of kaolin and flint, which is applied to the kiln shelves and floor to prevent fired glaze from adhering to them.

kneading Working clay on a surface with the palms of the hands in order to remove air from it and obtain a uniform consistency.

lag To provide additional insulation for the outside of a kiln.

lamellate See *flocs*. The microscopic plate-like formation which is characteristic of plastic clay.

leather-hard The condition of raw clay ware when most of the moisture has evaporated leaving it still soft enough to be carved or joined to other pieces.

levigation Refining dry clay by grinding with or without water.

long Very fat or plastic clay.

luster A type of metallic decoration applied to a glazed surface and then refired to a temperature just high enough to melt and fuse the metal to the glaze.

luting Joining leather-hard or dry clay with slip or vinegar.

majolica See *faïence*. Earthenware fired with a tin-lead glaze and decorated with a luster overglaze. The name derives from Majorca, the island where it purportedly was originated.

marl Clay which contains a considerable amount of lime.

matt The nonglossy surface quality of a completely fired glaze.

maturity The firing point at which glaze ingredients have reached complete fusion or when clay has reached maximum nonporosity and hardness.

mealy Crumbly, nonplastic, powdery, dry.

mishima A Japanese decorating method of filling a design impressed in clay with a different colored clay slip.

mold A plaster or bisqued clay shape from which a clay form can be reproduced.

mole The weight of a raw material needed in a glaze to give one molecule of an oxide when fired.

molecular formula A glaze formula expressing the relative proportions of its constituent compounds.

muffle The inner lining of a kiln which prevents flame from directly touching the ware.

muller A grinding machine with rollers used to prepare large batches of clay.

neat cement A mixture of calcinated clay and limestone without sand or other aggregate.

necking See *collaring*.

neutral atmosphere An atmosphere in a kiln between reduction and oxidation. This is only theoretically possible in a fuel kiln, but is the actual atmosphere present in an electric kiln where there is no flame.

oil spots See *temmoku*.

once fire or **single fire** A slow firing cycle which combines both bisque and glaze firings.

open A clay body that is porous in structure because of grain size, fillers or grog.

open firing A firing in which the flame touches the ware directly.

opacifier A substance whose small particles are relatively insoluble in a glaze. The reflectivity of these particles prevents light from penetrating the glass formation.

overglaze Glaze decoration applied on the surface of a fired glaze.

overglaze colors Colors containing coloring oxides or ceramic stains, flux and a binder used to decorate fired ware.

oxide A compound containing oxygen and other elements. Sometimes refers to metallic chemicals used for coloring clays or glazes.

oxidation fire A fire during which the kiln chamber retains an ample supply of oxygen.

parian ware a soft paste, unglazed porcelain developed in England during the nineteenth century in imitation of Greek white marble.

paste The European term for a white clay body.

pâte-sur-pâte A method of decoration which consists of building up a low relief with repeated layers of engobe. From the French, meaning "paste on paste."

peach bloom A Chinese copper-red reduction glaze with a peach-like pink color.

peeling Separation of the fired glaze or slip from a clay surface because the clay has contracted more than the glaze.

petuntze A partially decomposed feldspathic rock found in China. Used in glaze and in porcelain clay bodies.

pH The measure of the relative alkalinity or acidity of a solution.

pins Refractory supports used to place ware in racks or saggars for firing.

plaster of paris Calcined hydrated calcium sulfate, or gypsum, used in ceramics to make molds and bats.

plasticity The quality of clay that allows it to be easily manipulated and still maintain its shape.

porcelain A strong, vitreous, translucent, white clay body that matures at cone 12 or above.

porosity The capacity of a clay body to absorb moisture.

pressing The forming of clay objects by squeezing soft clay between two halves of a mold.

primary clay Clay found at the original site where it was formed by decomposing rock.

pug To mix clay with water to make it plastic.

pug mill A machine with a paddle gear for grinding and mixing plastic clay.

pyrometer A bi-metallic strip which translates heat energy into electrical energy used to indicate the temperature in a kiln. Optical pyrometers perform the same function but use color as the indicator.

pyrometric cone See *cone.*

raku A technique of rapidly firing low temperature glazed bisque ware. Raku means "enjoyment of leisure" or "contentment" and was the method used to make bowls for the Japanese tea ceremony.

raw Unfired, in a natural state.

red heat The firing temperature at which the interior of a kiln begins to glow.

reduction fire A fire in which the supply of oxygen is inadequate to promote complete combustion. The carbon monoxide thus formed combines with oxygen from clay and glazes, altering their colors.

refractory The quality of resistance to high temperatures. Also, high alumina-silica material used in the manufacture of kiln furniture and interiors.

residual clay See *primary clay.*

rib A hand held tool made of hard material used to shape a pot when throwing.

rouge flambé A Chinese copper-red reduction glaze. From the French, meaning "burnt red."

saddles Refractory props used between plates when stacked on edge in a kiln.

saggar or **sagger** A fireclay box which protects ware from flame and combustion gases during firing.

sagging The slumping of a form while the plastic clay is still soft.

sang de boeuf A Chinese copper-red reduction glaze. From the French, meaning "oxblood."

salt glaze To glaze raw ware by vapors from common salt introduced into the kiln during firing.

scaling Flaking or peeling of glaze.

secondary clay Clay that has been transported from its original site by water, air or ice and deposited in layers elsewhere.

sedimentary clay See *secondary clay.*

sgraffito A decorative process by which a line is scratched through a layer of slip or glaze before firing to expose the clay body beneath. From the Italian, meaning "scratched out."

shard or **sherd** A fragment of pottery.

short Clay that is nonplastic and breaks or crumbles easily.

shrinkage Contraction of the clay or glaze in either drying or firing.

siccative A substance which promotes the drying of oils used in underglazes or overglazes.

sinter To fire to the point where materials fuse sufficiently to form a solid mass upon cooling, but are not vitrified.

size or **sizing** A solution used to prevent poured plaster from adhering to a surface.

slake To pour dry material into liquid and allow it to absorb the liquid to its fullest capacity.

slip A suspension of clay or glaze materials in water.

slip clay A clay, such as Albany or Barnard, containing sufficient flux to become a glaze when fired to high temperatures.

slip glaze A glaze made chiefly from clay.

slip trailing A decorating method which uses a syringe to apply slip to a clay surface.

slurry A creamy mixture of clay and water.

soak To maintain the kiln at a particular temperature for a period of time.

soap A brick cut in half lengthwise to dimension of 9" x 2 1/2" x 2 1/4".

soluble Capable of being dissolved in liquid.

spall To chip or splinter off.

spare The excess clay which is trimmed off cast ware.

spinel Chemically, magnesium aluminate ($MgO \cdot Al_2O_3$). In ceramics, the term designates a large group of coloring materials with the formula $RO \cdot R_2O_3$.

sprig A mold-made ornament of plastic clay applied to a clay surface to form a relief decoration.

spurs Triangular refractory supports which keep glazed ware from touching kiln shelves during firing.

spy hole The opening in a kiln wall or door through which cones may be viewed during firing. Can also act as a steam vent during the early stages of firing.

stacking Efficient loading of a kiln with the maximum amount of ware.

stain A prepared calcined pigment used to color clay bodies or glazes.

stilt A ceramic tripod used to support glazed ware in a kiln during firing.

stoneware A grey to buff, nontranslucent clay body which matures between cones 6 and 10.

temmoku A rich purple-black Japanese glaze which may develop brownish "hare's fur" streaks or metallic "oil spots." The name comes from Tien-mu-Shan, "Mountain of the Eye of Heaven," a mountain in Chichiang province, China.

template A pattern placed against a clay form as a guide in shaping.

terra cotta A brownish-orange earthenware clay body, commonly used for ceramic sculpture or architectural ornament. From the Italian, meaning "baked earth."

terra sigillata Originally referred to Roman stamped ware, or Arretine ware. Has come to mean the thin slip coating on Roman and Greek ware. Made of fine particles of decanted clay, it is applied thinly over a clay surface and then fired to a low temperature. From the Italian, meaning "stamped earth."

throw or **throwing** Using the potter's wheel to make forms by hand from plastic clay.

throwing stick Long-handled spoon-shaped stick for shaping interior of tall narrow wheel thrown forms.

tin-enamel A lead glaze opacified by tin oxide.

tooth The quality of roughness in clay caused by its coarse grain structure or the addition of grog or other fillers.

trailing See *slip trailing*.

translucency The ability to transmit a diffused light.

trimming A method of paring away excess clay, usually from the bottom of a pot to form a foot, while the clay is leather-hard.

turning See *trimming*.

undercut The inward slant of a mold which can prevent clay from being released.

underglaze A colored decoration applied on raw or bisque ware before the glaze is applied.

viscosity The property of a liquid to resist movement.

vitreous The hard, glassy and nonabsorbent quality of a clay body or glaze.

vitrify or **vitrification** To fire to the temperature at which a clay or glaze attains its mature, hard, glass-like quality.

volatilize To pass off as a vapor.

warping Distortion of a clay shape caused by uneven stresses during shaping, drying or firing.

water glass The liquid solution of sodium silicate used as a deflocculant.

water smoking An early stage of a firing during which the chemically combined water evaporates from the clay.

wax resist Wax emulsion or melted wax which is used to prevent slips or glazes from adhering to a clay surface. Can also be used to retard the drying of leather-hard ware.

weathering The exposure of raw clay to the natural elements which break down the particle size and render the clay more plastic.

wedge or **wedging** Mixing and de-airing clay by cutting it diagonally and slamming the pieces together.

welding Joining pieces of soft or leather-hard clay.

wet firing A process by which freshly formed clay objects can be fired immediately without pre-drying.

whiteware Ware made from a white or light cream-colored clay body, usually fired to a low temperature.

Bibliography

Methods

Ball, F. Carlton and Lovoos, Janet. *Making Pottery Without a Wheel.* New York: Reinhold Publishing Company, 1965, 159 p. illus.

Berensohn, Paulus. *Finding One's Way with Clay: Pinched Pottery and the Color of Clay.* New York: Simon and Schuster, 1972, 159 p. illus.

Counts, Charles. *Pottery Workshop.* New York: Macmillan Publishing Company, Inc., 1973, 198 p. illus.

Dickerson, John. *Raku Handbook.* New York: Van Nostrand Reinhold Company, 1972, 112 p. illus.

Fox, James. "Dry Throwing," *Ceramics Monthly,* vol. 21, no. 8 (October, 1973), pp. 22-26.

Green, David. *Pottery: Materials and Techniques.* New York: Frederick A. Praeger, Publishers, 1967, 148 p. illus.

Kenny, John B. *Ceramic Design.* Philadelphia: Chilton Company, 1963, 322 p. illus.

Leach, Bernard. *A Potter's Book.* Eighth American edition. Hollywood-by-the-Sea, Florida: Transatlantic Arts, Inc., 1960, 294 p. illus.

Nelson, Glenn C. *Ceramics: A Potter's Handbook.* Third edition. New York: Holt, Rinehart and Winston, Inc., 1971, 348 p. illus.

Peipenburg, Robert. *Raku Pottery.* New York: The Macmillan Company, 1972, 159 p. illus.

Trevor, Henry. *Pottery Step-by-Step.* New York: Watson-Guptill Publications, 1966, 127 p. illus.

Young, Joseph. *Mosaics: Principles and Practice.* New York: Reinhold Publishing Corporation, 1963, 128 p. illus.

Design

Collier, Graham. *Form, Space and Vision.* Third edition. Englewood Cliffs, New Jersey: Prentice-Hall, Inc., 1972, 304 p. illus.

Feininger, Andreas. *Forms of Nature and Life.* New York: Viking Press, 1966, 172 p. illus.

Kepes, Gyorgy ed. *Vision and Value Series.* New York: George Braziller, 1965, 6 vols. illus.

Knobler, Nathan. *The Visual Dialogue.* New York: Holt, Rinehart and Winston, Inc., 1966, 342 p. illus.

Krantz, Stewart and Fisher, Robert. *The Design Continuum.* New York: Reinhold Publishing Corporation, 1966, 151 p. illus.

Neutra, Richard. *Survival Through Design.* Oxford University, 1954, 384 p.

Papanek, Victor. *Design for the Real World.* New York: Bantam Books, 1973, 378 p. illus.

Randel, Reino and Haines, Edward C. *Design in Three Dimensions.* Worcester, Massachusetts: Davis Publishing, Inc., 1965, 69 p. illus.

Von Eckart, Wolf. *A Place to Live.* New York: A Seymour Lawrence Book, Delacorte Press, 1967, 430 p. illus.

Historical and Contemporary Ceramics

Birks, Tony. *The Art of the Modern Potter.* London: Country Life Limited, 1967, 160 p. illus.

Cox, Warren E. *The Book of Pottery and Porcelain.* 2 vols. New York: Crown Publishers, 1945, 1158 p. illus.

Hatterer, Lawrence J. *The Artist in Society.* New York: Grove Press, Inc., 1965, 188 p.

Larousse Encyclopedia of Mythology. New York: Prometheus Press, 1960, 500 p. illus.

Leach, Bernard. *A Potter in Japan.* London: Faber and Faber, 1960, 246 p. illus.

Miki, Fumio. *Haniwa: The Clay Sculpture of Proto-Historic Japan.* Translated by Roy Andrew Miller. Rutland, Vermont: Charles E. Tuttle Company, 1960, 161 p. illus.

Read, Herbert. "The Origins of Form in Art," *The Man Made Object.* Gyorgy Kepes, ed. New York: George Braziller, Inc., 1966, pp. 30-49.

Sanders, Herbert H. *The World of Japanese Ceramics.* Tokyo: Kodansha International Limited, 1968, 267 p. illus.

Wildenhain, Marguerite. *Pottery: Form and Expression.* New York: Reinhold Publishing Company, 1969, 157 p. illus.

Materials Information

Andrew, A. I. *Ceramic Tests and Calculations.* New York: John Wiley and Sons, Inc., 1928, 172 p.

Ceramic Glazes as a Factor in Lead Poisoning. Prepared for the Department of Consumer and Corporate Affairs, Canada, by J. R. Hickman. Issued by Hazardous Products Division, Standards Branch (March, 1971), 3 p.

Ceramic Industry, vol. 76, no. 1 (January, 1961), 174 p.

Facts about Lead Glazes for Art Potters and Hobbyists. New York: Lead Industries Association, Inc., 1971, 12 p. illus.

Lawrence, W. G. *Ceramic Science for the Potter.* Philadelphia: Chilton Book Company, 1972, 239 p. illus.

Lead in Glazes. Prepared for the Department of Consumer and Corporate Affairs, Canada, by K. E. Bell. Issued by Hazardous Products Division, Standards Branch (March, 1971), 3 p.

Norton, F. H. *Ceramics for the Artist Potter.* Cambridge, Mass.: Addison-Wesley, 1956, 320 p. illus.

Rhodes, Daniel. *Clay and Glazes for the Potter.* Revised edition. Philadelphia: Chilton Book Company, 1973, 330 p. illus.

_____. *Stoneware and Porcelain: The Art of High-Fired Pottery.* Philadelphia: Chilton Book Company, 1959, 217 p. illus.

Shaw, Kenneth. *Ceramic Colors and Pottery Decoration.* New York: Frederick A. Praeger, Publishers, 1962, 189 p. illus.

Kiln Construction

Fraser, Harry. *Electric Kilns.* New York: Watson-Guptill Publications, 1974, 144 p. illus.

Rhodes, Daniel. *Kilns: Design, Construction and Operation.* Philadelphia: Chilton Book Company, 1968, 240 p. illus.

Soldner, Paul. *Kiln Construction.* New York: American Crafts Council, 1965, 32 p. illus.

Marketing

Goodman, Calvin J. *Marketing Art.* Los Angeles: Gee Tee Bee, 1972, 318 p.

"The Handcraft Business," *Small Business Reporter,* vol. 10, no. 8 (1972), 16 p.

Nelson, Norbert N. *Selling Your Crafts.* New York: Reinhold Publishing Company, 1967, 126 p.

Nigrosh, Leon. "The Craft Fair," *Craft Horizons,* vol. 32, no. 5 (October, 1972), pp. 51-66.

Taxes and the Craftsman. Prepared for Members of the American Craftsmen's Council by Sydney Prereau. New York: American Crafts Council, 1964, 33 p.

Appendix A Ceramic Raw Materials

ALUMINA, Al_2O_3, increases the viscosity, refractoriness and opacity of a glaze. Alumina also improves the tensile strength of a glaze as well as its hardness and resistance to chemicals. Used in small amounts, it will prevent recrystallization of a glaze upon cooling. When used in proportions from 1:4 up to 1:20 with silica, alumina regulates the oxygen ratio to control the surface quality of a glaze from a dry matt to a brilliant gloss. Alumina will also affect glaze color. Chrome oxides which usually gives green tones, will tend toward red in a high alumina glaze. The normal blue tones of cobalt oxide will give pink hues in the absence of alumina. Depending upon the firing temperature, alumina can be added to a glaze formula from 0.1 moles at cone 010 ($887°C/1629°F$) to 0.9 moles at cone 12 ($1306°C/2383°F$). The most common sources of alumina for glazing are feldspars, clay and pyrophillite. To increase refractoriness in a clay body, alumina can be added by using kaolins, ball clays, feldspars, or alumina hydrate.

ALUMINA HYDRATE, $Al_2O_3·3H_2O$, is used primarily in stacking and firing to prevent ware from sticking to kiln shelves. It is sometimes used in high temperature industrial ceramic bodies because of its fineness and purity.

AMBLYGONITE, $2LiF·Al_2O_3·P_2O_5$, is the highest lithia-containing mineral, having between 8 and 10 percent available. It acts as a strong flux with alkaline reactions at temperatures around cone 2 ($1142°C/2088°F$) to cone 6 ($1201°C/2194°F$) and promotes a high gloss. Because it contains fluoride and phosphoric oxide, amblygonite will also tend to opacify a glaze.

ANTIMONY OXIDE, Sb_2O_3, although an opacifying agent, is used chiefly in combination with lead compounds to derive a yellow colorant. This compound, commercially available as Naples Yellow, is poisonous.

APATITE, $CaF_2·9CaO·3P_2O_5$, is a natural source of calcium phosphate occasionally used in a glaze as an opacifier. It is used chiefly in commercial high temperature whiteware bodies.

ARSENIC OXIDE, As_2O_3, can be used in a glaze as an opacifer, but it is not as effective as tin oxide. It is very poisonous and should be avoided.

BARIUM CARBONATE, $BaO·CO_2$, is the primary source of barium oxide used to induce mattness in a glaze. It is a moderately active flux at temperatures around cone 6 ($1201°C/2194°F$) and higher. In the raw state, all barium compounds are poisonous.

BARIUM CHROMATE, $BaO·CrO_3$, is used to produce yellow to green colors in low temperature overglazes.

BARIUM OXIDE, BaO, is refractory. When used in amounts from 0.1 to 0.7 moles, it will produce increasing degrees of mattness in a glaze from a satin finish to a very rough, dry surface. Barium oxide is a moderately active flux at high temperatures but will also stabilize low temperature glazes in the presence of alumina and silica. Brilliant blue colors can be gained from copper in a high barium glaze. In high temperature reduction glazes, barium favors celadon green and iron blue colors. The major source of barium oxide is barium carbonate.

BENTONITE, $Al_2O_3·4SiO_2·9H_2O$, is a clay of volcanic origin. It is used as a plasticizer in clay and as a floatative in glaze. Because it has a high drying shrinkage, an addition of 1 to 3 percent should not be exceeded.

BISMUTH OXIDE, Bi_2O_3, is a strong flux which can be used in amounts similar to lead oxide without the poisonous effects. Bismuth oxide can induce stable yellow colors under reducing conditions around cone 6 ($1201°C/2194°F$). Prepared by calcining bismuth nitrate, it is often used as a flux in silver luster glazes.

BISMUTH SUBNITRATE, $BiONO_3·H_2O$, melts at very low temperatures around $260°C$ ($500°F$). It is used in making pearlescent luster glazes.

BONE ASH, $13CaO·4P_2O_5·CO_2$, is made from ground up calcined animal bones. It is used as a flux in low temperature glazes and as a minor opacifier. Because of natural bone variations, true bone ash does not have a constant composition. Preferable calcium materials are apatite and refined calcium phosphate.

BORAX, $Na_2O·2B_2O_3·10H_2O$, is soluble in water and can lose some of its water of crystallization during storage, affecting its weight. Care should be taken to store borax in airtight containers. Next to lead, borax is the chief flux for low temperature glazes. It brings about bright colors, reduced viscosity, and heals application defects. When used in a high fire glaze in amounts under 10 percent, borax can effect the same healing qualities. However, an excess of borax can bring about glaze defects. *Fused* or *Anhydrous Borax* is prepared by heating borax to a temperature of $735°C$ ($1355°F$). This drives out all the water leaving a compound of $Na_2O·2B_2O_3$ which is less apt to separate in a melting glaze and can be substituted for raw borax in a ratio of 53:100.

BORIC ACID, $B_2O_3 \cdot 3H_2O$, although soluble, is sometimes used to introduce boric oxide into a glaze when the sodium content of borax is not desired.

BORIC OXIDE, B_2O_3, is available in fused form as tiny glasslike pellets which are often used in frit batches. The borates help reduce glaze expansion and therefore help prevent crazing. Opalescence and mottled colors can be induced by the addition of boric oxide. Although the fused boric oxide is more stable than boric acid, it is still water soluble. The only natural source of insoluble boric oxide is colemanite.

CADMIUM SULFIDE, CdS, is used in low temperature glazes to produce yellow colors. Cadmium-selenium compounds give red and red-orange colors. Cadmium loses its color above cone 010 ($887°C/1629°F$) due to decomposition of the sulfide.

CALCIUM CHLORIDE, $CaCl_2$, is used as an electrolyte to flocculate glaze slips, that is, to thicken their consistency.

CALCIUM CARBONATE or **WHITING**, $CaO \cdot CO_2$, is a chief source of calcium oxide for glazing. Found naturally in the mineral calcite, marble and some chalks, it is used in moderate amounts as a flux in all temperature ranges.

CALCIUM OXIDE, CaO, because of its many desirable properties is usually used to some extent in most glazes from cone 010 ($887°C/1629°F$) upward. Calcium oxide, primarily a high temperature flux, will bring about a melt at low temperatures when combined with other fluxes. Glazes with calcium oxide in them are harder, more durable, less soluble, and have a lower expansion rate than glazes without it. The high refractory quality of calcium oxide will produce matt surface glazes when used in amounts above 0.4 moles. Calcium content does not readily affect glaze color, although combinations of calcium and zinc or calcium and chrome can produce pinks, while calcium and lead can give greens. In a high temperature reduction glaze, calcium oxide will help induce iron celadon greens. Chief sources of calcium oxide are whiting, colemanite, dolomite, bone ash, and wollastonite.

CAROLINA STONE is an altered granite produced in the United States to replace cornwall stone normally imported from England. It is used in a glaze as a substitution for feldspar and in a clay body instead of feldspar and china clay.

CHROME OXIDE, Cr_2O_3, is used in most glazes as a green colorant. In a high lead glaze below cone 08 ($945°C/1733°F$), chrome oxide can give brilliant red to red-orange colors. A soda-lead low-fire glaze will turn chrome oxide bright yellow. A zinc glaze will turn chrome to brown. A glaze with tin oxide and chrome in a ratio of 5:1 will give a pink hue. In most glazes a two percent addition of chrome oxide is sufficient to give a strong color. Chrome oxide in amounts of 40 percent or more is used in the formulation of black ceramic stains. Chrome oxide is slightly volatile above cone 5 ($1177°C/2151°F$) and can affect the colors of other nearby glazes in the kiln, especially those with tin. In reduction, chrome tends to go black.

CLAY, **CHINA CLAY**, or **KAOLIN**, $Al_2O_3 \cdot 2SiO_2 \cdot 2H_2O$, is used in amounts up to 0.3 moles as a source of alumina and silica. Clay aids in controlling viscosity and gives the raw glaze better dry strength. Because china clays are relatively pure, they do not affect glaze color. Ball and other clays can be used in a glaze, but their impurities can affect color and also lower the maturing point.

CALCINED CLAY, $Al_2O_3 \cdot 2SiO_2$, has been heated above red heat to drive off chemically combined water, to reduce its plasticity and to decrease shrinkage. Without this water the effective percentages of available alumina and silica per unit of weight are greatly increased over non-calcined clay. Equal results can therefore be had with approximately 14 percent less calcined clay.

COBALT CARBONATE, $CoO \cdot CO_2$, is a reliable blue colorant at all temperatures, and in both firing atmospheres. In an alkaline glaze, it gives a brilliant blue. In a magnesia glaze, cobalt carbonate tends towards purples and pinks. Additions of more than one percent of cobalt carbonate tend to give dark blue to black colors.

COBALT OXIDE, CoO, is the considerably stronger version of the blue colorant. Approximately one-half cobalt oxide is needed to derive colors similar to the carbonate. Cobalt oxide may need to be milled to reduce speckles in a glaze.

COBALT CHROMATE, $CoCrO_4$; **COBALT NITRATE**, $Co(NO_3)_2$; and **COBALT SULFATE**, $CoSO_4 \cdot 7H_2O$; are all water soluble and are used primarily for making low fire blue stains or luster glazess.

COLEMANITE or **GERSTLEY BORATE**, $2CaO \cdot 3B_2O_3 \cdot 5H_2O$, contains both calcium and boron. It is the only source of boric oxide that is insoluble except for commercial frits. Because boron melts at a low temperature, colemanite can be used as a low fire flux. It helps prevent crazing and acts as a mild opacifier. At higher temperatures, it can give an opalescent quality to a glaze along with brighter colors. True colemanite tends to be slightly soluble in water and can therefore flocculate a glaze if allowed to stand for a few days. The more commonly available gerstley borate is fritted and therefore does not do this as readily. Colemanite tends to vary in composition and new lots should undergo testing before being introduced into a glaze.

COPPER CARBONATE, $CuO \cdot CO_2$, is a major green colorant. Up to 5 percent addition of copper carbonate will give a glaze deepening shades of green. Above five percent, the glaze surface will become opaque metallic black. In a low temperature high alkaline glaze, copper carbonate produces a turquoise blue. A colemanite based glaze will give a similar but slightly subdued color. Used in a high temperature barium glaze, copper carbonate will produce blue to blue-green. Although when copper carbonate is used in a lead glaze, it gives soft warm green colors, it also releases up to ten times the amount of poisonous lead than might otherwise be freed. Such a glaze should therefore not be used on ware for food or drink. In a reduction glaze, copper carbonate in small amounts will give red colors. If one to three percent tin oxide is added, brighter reds can be achieved.

COPPER OXIDE, CuO, has one and one-half times more available copper than does copper carbonate. Above cone 8 ($1236°C/2257°F$) copper becomes volatile and can affect nearby glazes in a kiln.

CORNWALL STONE is a natural mineral containing feldspar, flint, clay, and other minerals. It is used primarily as a flux, but can also help reduce glaze shrinkage in the unfired and fired state. Because it is high in silica, the addition of cornwall stone increases both the melting point of a glaze and its viscosity. Cornwall stone has a varying composition, usually around 0.4 moles of potassium, 0.2 each of soda and calcium, 1.1 alumina and 8.3 silica. The remainder is made up of small amounts of other minerals. Glaze tests should be made each time a new lot of cornwall stone is used.

CROCUS MARTIS, FeO, is a coarse form of impure iron oxide which can be used to speckle a glaze.

CRYOLITE, $3NaF \cdot AlF_3$, is used mainly as flux in the manufacture of glass. It is a violent flux at higher temperatures, causing a glaze to pinhole and blister. With proper temperature control, a glaze containing cryolite can have colorations similar to alkaline fluxes but with interesting striations.

CULLET, $Na_2O \cdot CaO \cdot 2SiO_2$, is powdered glass which is sometimes used as a frit in a glaze batch to lower the melting point. It does not have a constant composition.

DOLOMITE, $CaO \cdot MgO \cdot 2CO_2$, is a natural mineral containing calcium oxide and magnesium oxide in an approximate ratio of 4:6. Although it is refractory, it is an effective flux alone at higher temperatures, and at lower temperatures when combined with alkaline fluxes. Dolomite will assist in forming a smooth buttery surface on a glaze and contribute to its durability. It can also be used in a clay body to increase its firing range.

FELDSPAR, $KNaO$, is an important mineral used as the principal flux in most high temperature glazes. Feldspars are natural frits made up of an alkaline portion, alumina and silica. Although rarely found in their pure state, there are three common forms of feldspar:

> soda feldspar (albite) $Na_2O \cdot Al_2O_3 \cdot 6SiO_2$
> calcium feldspar (anorthite) $CaO \cdot Al_2O_3 \cdot 2SiO_2$
> potash feldspar (microcline) $K_2O \cdot Al_2O_3 \cdot 6SiO_2$

These formulas are theoretical and do not take into consideration other compounds and impurities which may be present. In actual use, a chemical analysis of a feldspar is required to establish its exact formula. Many feldspars will become glaze when fired to temperatures above $1250°C/2282°F$. Glazes high in feldspar will tend to craze. Other fluxes should be added to prevent this. Potash feldspars form a harder glaze surface and decrease thermal expansion. Soda feldspars have a lower maturing temperature and promote brighter colors.

FLINT or **QUARTZ**, SiO_2, is the main source of silica for glazing. Adding flint to a glaze decreases its thermal expansion, adding it to a clay body increases thermal expansion. Used in a clay body, flint reduces dry and fired shrinkage and increases refractoriness.

FLUORSPAR or **CALCIUM FLUORIDE**, CaF_2, is used as an opacifier and flux in the glass industry. It has a somewhat limited use as a glaze flux because its fluoride content tends to react violently with silica at higher temperatures, causing pinholes or blisters. At lower temperatures fluorspar aids in even colorant dispersal and imparts a higher gloss than does an equal amount of calcium carbonate. If the temperature is carefully controlled, fluorspar can induce unusual copper blue colors. Fluorspar and strontium combinations may be adequate substitutions for lead in a glaze.

GALENA or **LEAD SULFIDE**, PbS, is the raw material for lead compounds. It has been used since pre-history as a crude but direct source for lead in glazing.

GOLD, Au, is a widely used metallic overglaze decoration when prepared as liquid bright gold, powder or paste gold, or liquid burnished gold. The most brilliant of these is liquid bright gold. In a suitably fluxed liquid, it can be brushed, poured, sprayed or stamped onto a glaze fired surface. Fired to a low temperature over a gloss glaze, the gold is bright and shining; on a matt surface, it tends toward yellow. Gold-tin solutions and gold-salt solutions can be made to give purple and rose pink luster glazes.

ILMENITE, $TiO_2 \cdot FeO$, is a high iron mineral containing titanium. In powdered form, one to three percent ilmenite will tend to opacify a glaze and darken its color. Granular ilmenite used in a glaze or clay body will produce a speckled appearance. In conjunction with other colorants, one percent granular ilmenite may give dark spots with gold halos.

IRON CHROMATE, $FeO \cdot CrO_3$, is used to produce brown underglaze colors. From two to five percent can be added to a glaze to produce light to dark browns. In a low temperature tin glaze, dark pink tones are possible. Iron chromate is a non-staining form of iron which can also be used to darken a clay body.

IRON OXIDE is commonly used in two forms: Ferrous Oxide, FeO, and Ferric Oxide, Fe_2O_3. The usual form of iron oxide in ceramics is ferric oxide, known as red iron oxide. It can be used as a brown colorant in both a clay body and a glaze, in amounts ranging from one to seven percent. Greater amounts of iron will tend to flux and effectively lower the maturing temperature of the clay or glaze. In a low temperature lead glaze, two to five percent iron oxide will give amber colors. In a higher temperature lead glaze, it will give warm tan to dark brown. In a high lead glaze, amounts in excess of seven percent will tend to crystallize into yellows and reds, forming an aventurine glaze. Zinc tends to muddy iron colors while tin turns them to cream tones. In reduction firing two percent or less of iron will give pale green colors known as celadons. If the glaze is opacified with calcium phosphate, one-half percent of iron can give a pale blue color. In a high soda-barium glaze, one to two percent iron can produce a rich yellow. Large amounts of iron oxide can bring about iron reds. Red iron oxide is a fine powder and will

easily stain everything it contacts. Ferrous oxide, known as black iron oxide, is a coarse form of powdered iron. Non-staining, it can be substituted for red iron oxide in somewhat smaller amounts because of its greater iron to oxygen ratio.

KAOLIN, $Al_2O_3 \cdot 2SiO_2 \cdot 2H_2O$, is the Chinese name for a high temperature white burning clay. See Clay.

A Note About Lead

Lead is an all pervading natural element. An average of 16 parts per million of lead is in the earth's crust and is found in soil the world over. Small quantities of lead are therefore unavoidably present in food and water. Industrial processes, auto emissions, and waste disposal emit tons of lead into the air each year. Although small doses of lead may slowly pass from the body, larger amounts remain, usually in bones. Eventually this can cause lead intoxication, permanent damage to brain or bones, and even death. Presently, about 15 to 20 ppm of lead in the bloodstream is accepted as the average adult accumulation, with 40 ppm considered dangerous. A simple blood test can indicate the amount of lead in the blood. Chemical therapy is available to reduce, if not eliminate, the amount of lead in the body.

For centuries lead has been a primary flux in glass and glaze. Its desirable properties of low fusability, brilliance, luster, and smoothness are not easily equalled by other fluxes. Properly fritted with other glaze materials into lead silicate or other forms, lead becomes virtually insoluble and safer to use in glazing. Firing a lead glaze to the proper temperature for which it is compounded will also help reduce the possibility of "free" lead remaining in the glaze or on its surface. When using lead compounds in the studio, adequate ventilation is desirable and an approved respirator mask should be worn. Firing of lead glazes should be done with good ventilation. The same procedures should be followed when working with silica, barium, cadmium, cobalt, or any other toxic substance.

A simple method of avoiding lead contamination in a glaze is not to use lead. Lead volatilizes and is no longer a usable flux above cone 6 (1201°C/2194°F).

LEAD ANTIMONY, $3PbO \cdot Sb_2O_5$, is known as Naples Yellow and used in a low temperature glaze to produce yellow colors. It is extremely poisonous.

LEAD CARBONATE or **WHITE LEAD**, $3PbO \cdot 2CO_2 \cdot H_2O$, is a major low temperature flux. Its relative purity, small particle size and ready fusability make it the most reasonable way to introduce lead into a glaze.

LEAD CHROMATE, $PbO \cdot CrO_3$, is a low temperature green colorant. When used with tin oxide, it will give pink. It is also used to produce coral red stains.

LEAD OXIDE as used in ceramics comes in two forms: Litharge, PbO; and Red Lead, Pb_3O_4. Litharge, or yellow lead, has a coarser particle size and contains less oxygen per unit of weight than red lead. Red lead is less expensive than white lead, but its characteristic color easily stains everything it contacts. Because of its higher lead content, red lead is often used in the preparation of frits.

LEAD SILICATES are commercial frits compounded to reduce the toxicity of lead. The two most common forms are Lead Monosilicate with a composition of approximately 84 percent PbO and 16 percent SiO_2, and Lead Bisilicate, composed of 65 percent PbO, 33 percent SiO_2 and 2 percent Al_2O_3.

LEAD SILICATE, HYDROUS, $3PbO \cdot 2SiO_2 \cdot H_2O$, is used as a replacement for white lead to prevent pinholing caused by CO_2 release.

LEPIDOLITE, $LiF \cdot KF \cdot Al_2O_3 \cdot 3SiO_2$, is a lithium mica used as flux in a high temperature glaze. It tends to heighten glaze colors and decrease brittleness and thermal expansion. Lepidolite is used in a clay body to increase tensile strength and lengthen firing range.

LIME, CaO, is not found in a pure state in nature. It is generally combined in calcite or limestone. It is most often introduced into a glaze through whiting.

LITHIUM CARBONATE, $Li_2O \cdot CO_2$, is a good source of lithium for fluxing a high temperature glaze. It gives the glaze a high gloss and bright color response. It allows greater amounts of alumina, silica and calcium to be used, which gives the glaze greater durability and stability. Lithium carbonate can also be used in a mid-range glaze in place of lead.

MAGNESIUM CARBONATE, $MgO \cdot CO_2$, supplies magnesium oxide as a refractory in a low fire glaze to make it more matt and opaque. Added to a higher temperature glaze, magnesium oxide acts as a flux which gives a smooth, buttery surface. Cobalt blues turn purple or pinkish in a high magnesium glaze.

MAGNESIUM SULFATE or **EPSOM SALTS**, $MgO \cdot SO_3 \cdot 7H_2O$, will help prevent a glaze from settling in its container. A tablespoon per thousand grams is usually sufficient.

MANGANESE CARBONATE, $MnO \cdot CO_2$, is used as a colorant in glazing. If more than five percent is used, the glaze may become subject to pinholes or blisters. In mid-temperature alkaline glaze, manganese carbonate can impart a blue-purple to plum color. Above cone 6 ($1201°C/2194°F$) colors tend toward brown.

MANGANESE DIOXIDE, MnO_2, acts in a manner similar to manganese carbonate. Because it is coarse grained, it tends to make dark specks and is therefore also used in clay bodies.

NEPHELINE SYENITE is an igneous rock having characteristics similar to a high soda feldspar. Its formula varies, but in general it has a ratio of 0.7 soda and 0.2 potash to 1.0 alumina and 4.5 silica. It has a lower melting point than many feldspars and is therefore a good flux for a mid-temperature glaze as well as at higher temperatures. Nepheline syenite increases thermal expansion and can help eliminate crazing. It is also used in a clay body to increase its firing range and strength as well as decrease absorption. Fired shrinkage, however, is slightly increased.

NICKEL OXIDE is available in two forms: Green Nickel Oxide, NiO, and Black Nickel Oxide, Ni_2O_3. Amounts of nickel oxide around one percent can be used to moderate other colorants. By itself, nickel oxide will generally give grey to brown colors. Depending upon which fluxes are used and the amount of alumina in a base glaze, nickel colors can range from green with magnesia, brown with barium, to blue to brown with decreasing amounts of zinc. In barium-calcium combinations, it is possible to get purple to pink colors.

OCHRE is the name for a number of iron bearing surface clays which are used as glaze or slip colorants. They range in color from tans to brown or black.

PEARL ASH or **POTASSIUM CARBONATE**, $K_2O \cdot CO_2$, is soluble but may be used to alter colors produced by some colorants such as copper oxide. It is more often used as a potassium source for frits.

PETALITE, $Li_2O \cdot Al_2O_3 \cdot 8SiO_2$, is a source for lithia and silica in a mid- or high-temperature glaze. It can also be used effectively as a flux for a once-fired glaze. When fired above $1000°C$ ($1832°F$), petalite goes through decomposition and becomes beta spodumene. Used in a clay body, this unique feature offers nearly zero expansion and excellent heat shock resistance.

PLASTIC VITROX, a mineral similar in activity to potash feldspar and cornwall stone, is used as a source of silica, potash and alumina in a glaze.

PLATINUM, Pt, used as liquid bright platinum gives an overglaze luster color brighter than silver which is also less apt to tarnish. If added into a glaze, platinum gives a steel grey color.

POTASSIUM DICHROMATE, $K_2O \cdot 2CrO_3$, although soluble and poisonous, can be used in a low temperature glaze to give colors ranging from green to pink and red. For the latter, it is usually calcined with tin.

POTASSIUM NITRATE or **NITRE**, $K_2O \cdot N_2O_5$, because it is soluble, is usually introduced in fritted form as a source of potassium when a potash feldspar is not usable.

PRASEODYMIUM OXIDE, Pr_6O_{11}, is a rare earth useful as a brilliant yellow colorant in ceramic stains.

PYROPHYLLITE, $Al_2O_3 \cdot 4SiO_2 \cdot H_2O$, decreases cracking, shrinking and warping of a ceramic body while increasing its firing range. It is relatively nonplastic and is used mostly in wall tile clays. Because pyrophyllite increases the ability of both clay body and glaze to withstand sudden temperature changes, it can be used in amounts up to 25 percent as a clay body constituent for range-top cookware.

RUTILE, TiO_2, is an impure form of titanium oxide containing iron, chrome and vanadium. In powdered form, it is used primarily as a tan colorant or to opacify and mottle a glaze. In the granular form, rutile will tend to give brown specks or streaks. In conjunction with other colorants, rutile will give variegated textures and colors. It is also used to color clay.

SELENIUM, Se, is used mainly in the glass industry as a colorant which when combined with other oxides can produce a range of color through half the spectrum. In a very low temperature glaze, selenium can give reds and oranges. Somewhat richer colors are possible when selenium and cadmium are combined as a glaze stain. Selenium should not be used on tableware because in contact with food acids it could be toxic.

SILICA, SiO_2, comes in many different forms. The one most commonly used in ceramics is finely ground quartzite, called *Potters' Flint*. Silica forms a hard glass when fired to its melting point of $1750°C$ ($3182°F$). Silica is the major acid in the RO_2 group. By varying its ratio to the RO group, the melting point of a particular glaze can be closely controlled. In glaze batches, silica is generally added as a mineral combined in clay, feldspar or other materials.

SILICON CARBIDE, SiC, is used in the manufacture of high temperature kiln shelves and other refractory parts. Introduced into a glaze as fine ground particles, silicon carbide can act as a local reduction agent.

SILLIMANITE, $Al_2O_3 \cdot SiO_2$, is used as a constituent of high temperature refractory bodies such as those used in kiln furniture and fire bricks. It can be introduced into clay bodies in small amounts to aid in controlling volume.

SILVER CARBONATE, Ag_2CO_3, becomes an overglaze luster when used in a low temperature glaze which undergoes light reduction resulting in metallic silver.

SILVER CHLORIDE, AgCl, is used as a metallic silver overglaze when mixed with bismuth in a lead glaze and fired in reduction.

SILVER NITRATE, $AgNO_3$, mixed with resin and lavender oil and applied directly to a fired glaze surface will give a silver-yellow metallic luster when fired.

SODA ASH or **SODIUM CARBONATE**, $Na_2O \cdot CO_2$, is a very active, but soluble, flux. It is usually added to a glaze in fritted form. In small amounts, soda ash acts as a deflocculant in a clay slip and can be used as a suspender in engobes.

SODIUM ALUMINATE, $Na_2O \cdot Al_2O_3$, is sometimes substituted for soda ash as a clay slip deflocculant, to increase slip stability and dry strength.

SODIUM ANTIMONATE, $Na_2O \cdot Sb_2O_5 \cdot 7H_2O$, has better stability than antimony oxide and is therefore used to a greater extent in the preparation of yellow ceramic stains. It is poisonous.

SODIUM BICARBONATE or **BICARBONATE OF SODA**, $Na_2O \cdot H_2O \cdot 2CO_2$, is used to some extent as a sodium compound in the formulation of ceramic stains. It can be used as a non-poisonous alternative to sodium chloride for salt glazing. It also acts as a deflocculant in clay or glaze slips.

SODIUM CHLORIDE or **COMMON SALT**, NaCl, vaporizes when introduced directly into a hot kiln. The vapor forms a soda-silicate glaze on the exposed surfaces of the ware being fired. The process is known as salt glazing.

SODIUM NITRATE, $Na_2O \cdot N_2O_5$, is an expensive sodium compound used chiefly as an oxidizer in frit preparations.

SODIUM SILICATE or **WATER GLASS**, $Na_2O \cdot XSiO_2$, has a silica content that can vary from 1.0 to 4.0 depending upon the manufacturer's requirements. The higher the silica content, the stronger the sodium silicate will act as a clay slip deflocculant.

SODIUM URANATE, $Na_2O \cdot UO_3$, is a low temperature colorant. When combined with zirconium in a high soda glaze, it gives a yellow color; with tin, orange; and in an alumina-free high lead glaze, bright red.

SPINEL, $MgO \cdot Al_2O_3$, is a natural mineral with high refractory qualities. However, the term "spinel" more generally designates a wide group of compounds with the molecular structure, $RO \cdot R_2O_3$. These spinels are used as stable colorants in underglaze and clay body stains.

SPODUMENE, $Li_2O \cdot Al_2O_3 \cdot 4SiO_2$, is a major source of lithium in glaze and clay bodies. Spodumene is an active flux at higher temperatures and will develop bright copper blue colors. Used in a whiteware or flameware clay body, spodumene undergoes an irreversible expansion which reduces shrinkage when fired. Using spodumene it is possible to develop a nonplastic clay body with zero shrinkage.

STRONTIUM CARBONATE, $SrO \cdot CO_2$, is an active flux that can be used to replace lead in a glaze. It will raise the maturing point of the glaze, decrease its fluidity, and increase it thermal expansion. Strontium carbonate can also be used to replace zinc or calcium. In both cases, the glaze fit is improved, solubility is lowered, and hardness increased. In a clay body, replacing calcium or zinc with strontium carbonate will reduce pitting, pinholing, and blistering of applied glazes. At high temperatures, strontium carbonate lowers shrinkage, increases strength, and lowers porosity.

TALC, $3MgO \cdot 4SiO_2 \cdot H_2O$, is used in a glaze for both its magnesia and silica content. It is both a mild flux and opacifier. Talc is often used as a flux in a low temperature clay body. In a high temperature clay body, talc imparts high thermal and electrical shock resistance. In both high and low bodies, talc decreases moisture expansion, thereby reducing or eliminating delayed glaze crazing. Talc varies in composition and should be tested for lime content before it is used in a clay body. The higher the talc content, the better strength, lower absorption and lesser tendency to cause glaze shivering.

TIN OXIDE, SnO_2, is the most effective opacifier of all. One or two percent will opacify a glaze and improve its gloss. Normally about five percent of tin oxide added to a glaze will completely opacify it. Because of its increasing cost, tin is being replaced as an opacifier by zirconia materials. They do not give the smooth texture imparted by tin, nor do they favor chrome pink and vanadium yellow as does tin. Tin oxide is also used in the preparation of glaze and clay body stains. It will slightly lower the expansion of a glaze in which it is used.

TITANIUM DIOXIDE, TiO_2, is used as an opacifier when added to a glaze or underglaze. Two or three percent can give a milky opalescence. In higher amounts, it tends to form matt surface textures. In some zinc glazes, iron browns can become bright greens with the addition of titanium dioxide. In local reduction, titanium can give blue colors.

URANIUM OXIDE, U_3O_8, is a yellow to red-orange colorant when used in low temperature oxidation glazes.

VANADIUM PENTOXIDE, V_2O_5, is used as a colorant to produce yellow to brown hues. In reduction, it is possible to obtain green colors with vanadium pentoxide. It is a relatively weak colorant and must be used in amounts from six to ten percent to gain a pronounced color. Larger amounts tend to affect surface texture. Generally, vanadium is introduced into a glaze in the form of a vanadium-tin stain which produces stronger yellows than vanadium pentoxide alone.

VOLCANIC ASH consists of minute particles of volcanic glass. It can be used as a mid-range flux equalling approximately 70 percent feldspar and 30 percent flint. Its iron content will darken a glaze somewhat. In a low temperature clay body, volcanic ash will produce less warping, greater strength, and a longer firing range. Its composition and properties are variable and each new lot should be tested.

WOLLASTONITE, $CaO \cdot SiO_2$, is a natural calcium silicate used as a glaze flux. As a source of calcium it tends to produce a smoother, brighter glaze than does whiting. When used in a clay body, wollastonite will reduce shrinkage, improve heat shock resistance, and lower moisture expansion.

ZINC OXIDE, ZnO, is a glaze flux which improves gloss, reduces crazing, increases the firing range, and heightens colors. Combined with alumina in a low calcium glaze, zinc oxide produces an opaque white matt glaze known as Bristol. Copper and zinc produce brilliant turquoise greens; zinc and tin can give pink; and zinc with iron or chrome makes brown tones. When used with titanium, zinc can promote a crystalline glaze. Large amounts of zinc oxide in a glaze will render it too refractory and cause crawling, pitting and pinholing. The use of Calcined Zinc Oxide will help prevent this.

ZIRCONIUM OXIDE, ZrO_2, functions as an opacifier at all temperatures. It is available in various fritted silicate forms such as Calcium Zirconium Silicate, Magnesium Zirconium Silicate, and silicates marketed as Zircopax, Superpax, Opax and others. Although these products are less expensive than tin oxide, twice as much of the material is usually needed to achieve the same opacity.

Appendix B Atomic Weights of Common Elements and Their Oxides

Element	Symbol	Atomic Weight	Oxide	Atomic Weight
Aluminum	Al	26.98	Al_2O_3	101.93
Antimony	Sb	121.75	Sb_2O_3	291.47
Arsenic	As	74.92	As_2O_3	197.81
Barium	Ba	137.34	BaO	153.33
Bismuth	Bi	208.90	Bi_2O_3	465.77
Boron	B	10.81	B_2O_3	69.59
Cadmium	Cd	112.40	CdO	128.39
Calcium	Ca	40.08	CaO	56.07
Carbon	C	12.01	CO_2	43.99
Chlorine	Cl	35.35	ClO_2	67.43
Chromium	Cr	51.99	Cr_2O_3	151.95
Cobalt	Co	58.93	CoO	74.92
Copper	Cu	63.54	CuO	79.53
Fluorine	F	18.99	—	
Gold	Au	196.96	Au_2O_3	441.89
Hydrogen	H	1.00	H_2O	17.99
Iron	Fe	55.84	FeO	71.83
			Fe_2O_3	159.65
Lead	Pb	207.19	PbO	223.18
Lithium	Li	6.93	Li_2O	29.85
Magnesium	Mg	24.31	MgO	40.30
Manganese	Mn	54.93	MnO	70.92
Mercury	Hg	200.61	HgO	216.60
Molybdenum	Mo	95.95	MoO_2	127.93
Nickel	Ni	58.71	NiO	74.70
Nitrogen	N	14.00	N_2O	43.99
Oxygen	O	15.99	—	
Palladium	Pd	106.40	PdO	122.39
Phosphorus	P	30.93	P_2O_5	141.81
Platinum	Pt	195.09	PtO	211.08
Potassium	K	39.10	K_2O	94.19
Praseodymium	Pr	140.90	Pr_6O_{11}	1021.29
Selenium	Se	78.96	SeO_2	110.94
Silicon	Si	28.08	SiO_2	60.06
Silver	Ag	107.87	Ag_2O	231.73
Sodium	Na	22.98	Na_2O	61.95
Strontium	Sr	87.62	SrO	103.61
Sulphur	S	32.06	SO_2	64.04
Tin	Sn	118.69	SnO_2	150.67
Titanium	Ti	47.90	TiO_2	79.88
Uranium	U	238.07	UO_3	286.04
			U_3O_8	842.13
Vanadium	V	50.94	V_2O_5	181.85
Zinc	Zn	65.37	ZnO	81.36
Zirconium	Zr	91.22	ZrO_2	123.20

Appendix C Ceramic Raw Materials—Formula and Weight Charts

Material	Raw Formula	Molecular Weight	Calculation Formula	Equivalent Weight
Alumina Hydrate	$Al_2O_3 \cdot 3H_2O$	156	Al_2O_3	156
Amblygonite	$2LiF \cdot Al_2O_3 \cdot P_2O_5$	296	$2Li_2O \cdot Al_2O_3$	162
Barium Carbonate	$BaO \cdot CO_2$	197	BaO	197
Bismuth Oxide	Bi_2O_3	466	Bi_2O_3	466
Bone Ash	$13CaO \cdot 4P_2O_5 \cdot CO_2$	1340	CaO	103
Borax	$Na_2O \cdot 2B_2O_3 \cdot 10H_2O$	381	$Na_2O \cdot 2B_2O_3$	381
Boric Acid	$B_2O_3 \cdot 3H_2O$	124	B_2O_3	124
Clay (Kaolin, China Clay)	$Al_2O_3 \cdot 2SiO_2 \cdot 2H_2O$	258	$Al_2O_3 \cdot 2SiO_2$	258
Calcined Clay	$Al_2O_3 \cdot 2SiO_2$	222	$Al_2O_3 \cdot 2SiO_2$	222
Calcium Phosphate	$3CaO \cdot P_2O_5$	310	CaO	103
Colemanite (Gerstley Borate)	$2CaO \cdot 3B_2O_3 \cdot 5H_2O$	411	$CaO \cdot 1.5B_2O_3$	206
Cryolite	$3NaF \cdot AlF_3$	210	$3Na_2O \cdot Al_2O_3$	420
Cullet	$Na_2O \cdot CaO \cdot 2SiO_2$	238	$Na_2O \cdot CaO \cdot 2SiO_2$	238
Dolomite	$CaO \cdot MgO \cdot 2CO_2$	184	$CaO \cdot MgO$	184
Flint (Silica, Quartz)	SiO_2	60	SiO_2	60
Fluorspar (Calcium Fluoride)	CaF_2	78	CaO	78
Galena (Lead Sulfide)	PbS	239	PbS	239
Lead Carbonate (White Lead)	$3PbO \cdot 2CO_2 \cdot H_2O$	776	PbO	259
Lead Monosilicate	$3PbO \cdot 2SiO_2$	790	$3PbO \cdot 2SiO_2$	263
Lead Oxide (Litharge)	PbO	223	PbO	223
Lead Oxide (Red Lead)	Pb_3O_4	686	PbO	229
Lepidolite	$LiF \cdot KF \cdot Al_2O_3 \cdot 3SiO_2$	366	$Li_2O \cdot K_2O \cdot Al_2O_3 \cdot 3SiO_2$	406
Lithium Carbonate	$Li_2O \cdot CO_2$	74	Li_2O	74
Magnesium Carbonate	$MgO \cdot CO_2$	84	MgO	84
Pearl Ash (Potassium Carbonate)	$K_2O \cdot CO_2$	138	K_2O	138
Petalite	$Li_2O \cdot Al_2O_3 \cdot 8SiO_2$	612	$Li_2O \cdot Al_2O_3 \cdot 8SiO_2$	612
Potassium Nitrate (Nitre)	$K_2O \cdot N_2O_5$	101	K_2O	202
Pyrophyllite	$Al_2O_3 \cdot 4SiO_2 \cdot H_2O$	360	$Al_2O_3 \cdot 4SiO_2$	360
Soda Ash (Sodium Carbonate)	$Na_2O \cdot CO_2$	106	Na_2O	106
Sodium Bicarbonate	$Na_2O \cdot H_2O \cdot 2CO_2$	168	Na_2O	168
Sodium Chloride	$NaCl$	58	Na_2O	117
Sodium Nitrate	$Na_2O \cdot N_2O_5$	170	Na_2O	170
Spodumene	$Li_2O \cdot Al_2O_3 \cdot 4SiO_2$	372	$Li_2O \cdot Al_2O_3 \cdot 4SiO_2$	372

Material	Raw Formula	Molecular Weight	Calculation Formula	Equivalent Weight
Strontium Carbonate	$SrO \cdot CO_2$	148	SrO	148
Talc	$3MgO \cdot 4SiO_2 \cdot H_2O$	379	$MgO \cdot 1.33SiO_2$	126
Whiting (Calcium Carbonate)	$CaO \cdot CO_2$	100	CaO	100
Wollastonite	$CaO \cdot SiO_2$	116	$CaO \cdot SiO_2$	116
Zinc Oxide	ZnO	81	ZnO	81

Colorants and Opacifiers

Material	Raw Formula	Molecular Weight	Calculation Formula	Equivalent Weight
Antimony Oxide	Sb_2O_3	292	Sb_2O_3	292
Apatite	$CaF_2 \cdot 9CaO \cdot 3P_2O_5$	1008	CaO	101
Arsenic Oxide	As_2O_3	198	As_2O_3	198
Barium Chromate	$BaO \cdot CrO_3$	253	$BaO \cdot CrO_3$	253
Cadmium Sulfide	CdS	144	Cd	112
Chrome Oxide	Cr_2O_3	152	Cr_2O_3	152
Cobalt Carbonate	$CoO \cdot CO_2$	119	CoO	119
Cobalt Oxide, Grey	CoO	75	CoO	75
Cobalt Oxide, Black	Co_3O_4	241	CoO	80
Copper Carbonate	$CuO \cdot CO_2$	124	CuO	124
Copper Oxide, Black	CuO	80	CuO	80
Copper Oxide, Red	Cu_2O	143	CuO	72
Ilmenite	$TiO_2 \cdot FeO$	152	$TiO_2 \cdot FeO$	152
Iron Chromate	$FeO \cdot CrO_3$	172	$FeO \cdot CrO_3$	172
Iron Oxide, Black	FeO	72	FeO	72
Iron Oxide, Red	Fe_2O_3	160	Fe_2O_3	160
Lead Antimony	$3PbO \cdot Sb_2O_5$	993	$3PbO \cdot Sb_2O_5$	993
Lead Chromate	$PbO \cdot CrO_3$	323	$PbO \cdot CrO_3$	323
Manganese Carbonate	$MnO \cdot CO_2$	115	MnO	115
Manganese Dioxide	MnO_2	87	MnO	87
Nickel Oxide, Green	NiO	75	NiO	75
Nickel Oxide, Black	Ni_2O_3	165	NiO	83
Potassium Dichromate	$K_2O \cdot 2CrO_3$	294	$K_2O \cdot 2CrO_3$	294
Praseodymium Oxide	Pr_6O_{11}	1021	Pr_6O_{11}	1021
Rutile	TiO_2	80	TiO_2	80
Selenium	Se	79	Se	79
Sodium Antimonate	$Na_2O \cdot Sb_2O_5 \cdot 7H_2O$	512	$Na_2O \cdot Sb_2O_5$	512
Sodium Uranate	$Na_2O \cdot UO_3$	348	$Na_2O \cdot UO_3$	348
Tin Oxide	SnO_2	151	SnO_2	151
Titanium Dioxide	TiO_2	80	TiO_2	80
Uranium Oxide	U_3O_8	842	U_3O_8	842
Vanadium Pentoxide	V_2O_5	182	V_2O_5	182
Zirconium Oxide	ZrO_2	123	ZrO_2	123
Zirconium Silicate	$ZrSiO_4$	183	$ZrSiO_4$	183

Typical Feldspar Formulas

All feldspars should have their chemical analyses changed into formulas and be test fired before being introduced into glazes or clay bodies. The following formulas are representative of analyses current to the publication date.

Spar	K_2O	Na_2O	CaO	MgO	CaF_2	Fe_2O_3	Al_2O_3	SiO_2	LOI	Equivalent Weight
Albite (theoretical)		1.0					1.0	6.0		524
Anorthite (theoretical)			1.0				1.0	2.0		278
Microcline (theoretical)	1.0						1.0	6.0		556
Feldspar Corp. K-200	.83	.15	.02			.003	1.08	6.67	.26	599
Cornwall Stone	.49	.26	.20	.01	.04	.006	1.15	8.28	1.25	692
Plastic Vitrox	.61	.34	.05				1.33	13.90		1051
Kona F-4	.31	.49	.20			.001	1.01	5.56	.20	508
Custer	.67	.29	.03			.003	1.04	6.95	.30	606
Nepheline Syenite	.24	.74	.02			.002	.99	4.36	.40	432

Appendix D Clay and Glaze Recipes

The following clay and glaze recipes are offered as general examples. Actual results may vary depending upon local materials used. Samples should be made and tested before any formulas are mixed in large amounts.

Clay Bodies

Raku

Fireclay	50	Stoneware	20
Ball Clay	50	Fireclay	35
+ Grog 20-50%		Talc	10
		Sand	35

Cone 04 Oxidation

White		Red	
Stoneware	30	Earthenware	60
China Clay	25	Ball Clay	25
Flint	15	Talc	10
Frit	15	Soda Ash	5
Nepheline Syenite	5	(self glazes in reduction.)	
Talc	10		

Cone 4 to 6 Oxidation

Tan		Tan	
Earthenware	50	Red Stoneware	50
Fireclay	20	Stoneware	33
Flint	15	Fireclay	17
Ball Clay	15	+ Grog 10%	

Cone 8 to 10 Oxidation or Reduction

White		Dark	
China Clay	25	Earthenware	20
Ball Clay	25	Stoneware	20
Flint	25	Fireclay	40
Feldspar	25	Ball Clay	20
		+ Feldspar 2%	

Glazes

Raku

White Reduction		*Chrome Red Oxidation*		*White Oxidation*	
Gerstley Borate	80	White Lead	77	Red Lead	85
Nepheline Syenite	20	China Clay	7	Flint	15
		Flint	14	+ Tin Oxide 10%	
		Chrome Oxide	2		

Orange 2% Potassium Dichromate
Yellow   1% Lead Chromate
Green   3% Copper Oxide

Cone 04 Oxidation

Gloss		*Matt*		*Flame Red Crystalline*	
Gerstley Borate	39	Potash Feldspar	38	Red Lead	63
China Clay	18	Gerstley Borate	22	Potassium Dichromate	4
Flint	40	Barium Carbonate	4	Chrome Oxide	3
		Whiting	11	Soda Ash	7
		Flint	25	China Clay	9
				Flint	7
				Tin Oxide	7

Cone 4 Oxidation

Gloss		*Matt*		*Satin Matt*	
Soda Feldspar	44	Potash Feldspar	52	Lepidolite	36
Gerstley Borate	19	Whiting	19	Wollastonite	26
Dolomite	6	Zinc Oxide	9	Barium Carbonate	18
Whiting	2	China Clay	15	Magnesium Carbonate	3
Zinc Oxide	5	Flint	5	Zinc Oxide	4
China Clay	5			Flint	13
Flint	19				

Cone 6 Oxidation

Gloss		*Matt*		*Semi Matt*	
Nepheline Syenite	47	Potash Feldspar	53	Nepheline Syenite	60
Gerstley Borate	27	Barium Carbonate	20	Barium Carbonate	22
China Clay	6	Whiting	10	Lithium Carbonate	4
Flint	20	Zinc Oxide	12	China Clay	8
		China Clay	5	Flint	6

Cone 8 Oxidation

Gloss		Matt	
Soda Feldspar	52	Soda Feldspar	56
Zinc Oxide	14	Nepheline Syenite	15
Bone Ash	7	Barium Carbonate	7
China Clay	7	Whiting	13
Flint	20	China Clay	9

Cone 10 Reduction

Gloss		Matt		Semi Matt	
Feldspar	33	Nepheline Syenite	26	Soda Feldspar	40
Cornwall Stone	32	Dolomite	14	Talc	20
Dolomite	11	Zinc Oxide	22	Whiting	10
Whiting	11	Whiting	1	China Clay	10
China Clay	3	China Clay	5	Flint	20
Flint	10	Flint	32		

Kiln Repair Paste

One part each: Ball Clay
China clay
Flint
Feldspar

Mix with liquid Sodium Silicate. Mend broken part, let dry, fire.

Appendix E Solutions to Glaze Problems

Problem A

Material	Calculation formula	Moles	Oxides in Formula Moles in Formula	K₂O .4	Na₂O .4	CaO .2	Al₂O₃ .35	SiO₂ 2.5
Pearl Ash	K_2O	.4		.4				
Soda Ash	Na_2O	.4			.4			
Whiting	CaO	.2				.2		
Clay	$Al_2O_3 \cdot 2SiO_2$	.35					.35	.7
Flint	SiO_2	1.8						1.8
			Total	.4	.4	.2	.35	2.5

Material	Moles	X	Equivalent Weight	=	Weight Factor	X	Key	=	% Batch
Pearl Ash	.4	x	138	=	55.2	x	.3166	=	17.476
Soda Ash	.4	x	106	=	42.4	x	.3166	=	13.423
Whiting	.2	x	100	=	20.0	x	.3166	=	6.332
Clay	.35	x	258	=	90.3	x	.3166	=	28.588
Flint	1.8	x	60	=	108.0	x	.3166	=	34.192
				$100 \div \overline{315.9} = .3166$					100.011

Problem B

Material	Calculation Formula	Moles	Oxides in Formula Moles in Formula	Na_2O .3	BaO .3	CaO .2	ZnO .2	Al_2O_3 .38	SiO_2 4.30
Soda Ash	Na_2O	.3		.3					
Barium Carbonate	BaO	.3			.3				
Whiting	CaO	.2				.2			
Zinc Oxide	ZnO	.2					.2		
Clay	$Al_2O_3 \cdot 2SiO_2$	.38						.38	.76
Flint	SiO_2	3.54							3.54
			Total	.3	.3	.2	.2	.38	4.30

Material	Moles	X	Equivalent Weight	=	Weight Factor	X	Key	=	% Batch
Soda Ash	.3	x	106	=	31.8	x	.2286	=	7.269
Barium Carbonate	.3	x	197	=	59.1	x	.2286	=	13.510
Whiting	.2	x	100	=	20.0	x	.2286	=	4.572
Zinc Oxide	.2	x	81	=	16.2	x	.2286	=	3.703
Clay	.38	x	258	=	98.04	x	.2286	=	22.411
Flint	3.54	x	60	=	212.4	x	.2286	=	48.554
					$100 \div 437.54 = .2286$				100.019

Problem C

Material	Calculation Formula	Moles	Oxides in Formula / Moles in Formula	CaO	Na$_2$O	BaO	MgO	ZnO	Al$_2$O$_3$	SiO$_2$
				.3	.3	.2	.1	.1	.34	2.60
Anorthite	CaO·Al$_2$O$_3$·2SiO$_2$	.3		.3					.30	.60
Soda Ash	Na$_2$O	.3			.3					
Barium Carbonate	BaO	.2				.2				
Magnesium Carbonate	MgO	.1					.1			
Zinc Oxide	ZnO	.1						.1		
Clay	Al$_2$O$_3$·2SiO$_2$	.04							.04	.08
Flint	SiO$_2$	1.92								1.92
			Total	.3	.3	.2	.1	.1	.34	2.60

Material	Moles	X	Equivalent Weight	=	Weight Factor	X	Key	=	% Batch
Anorthite	.3	x	278	=	83.4	x	.3371	=	28.114
Soda Ash	.3	x	106	=	31.8	x	.3371	=	10.720
Barium Carbonate	.2	x	197	=	39.4	x	.3371	=	13.282
Magnesium Carbonate	.1	x	84	=	8.4	x	.3371	=	2.832
Zinc Oxide	.1	x	81	=	8.1	x	.3371	=	2.731
Clay	.04	x	258	=	10.32	x	.3371	=	3.479
Flint	1.92	x	60	=	115.20	x	.3371	=	38.834
					100 ÷ 296.62 = .3371				99.992

Problem D

Material	Calculation Formula	Moles	Oxides in Formula / Moles in Formula	Na_2O	CaO	MgO	BaO	Al_2O_3	SiO_2
				.4	.3	.2	.1	.45	3.4
Albite	$Na_2O \cdot Al_2O_3 \cdot 6SiO_2$	.4		.4				.40	2.4
Dolomite	$CaO \cdot MgO$	.2			.2	.2			
Whiting	CaO	.1			.1				
Barium Carbonate	BaO	.1					.1		
Clay	$Al_2O_3 \cdot 2SiO_2$	.05						.05	.1
Flint	SiO_2	9							.9
			Total	.4	.3	.2	.1	.45	3.4

Material	Moles	X	Equivalent Weight	=	Weight Factor	X	Key	=	% Batch
Albite	.4	x	524	=	209.6	x	.2915	=	61.098
Dolomite	.2	x	184	=	36.8	x	.2915	=	10.727
Whiting	.1	x	100	=	10.0	x	.2915	=	2.915
Barium Carbonate	.1	x	197	=	19.7	x	.2915	=	5.743
Clay	.05	x	258	=	12.9	x	.2915	=	3.760
Flint	.9	x	60	=	54.0	x	.2915	=	15.741
					$100 \div 343 = .2915$				99.984

Problem E

$$\frac{.35B_2O_3}{2\,B_2O_3} = 0.175 \quad \text{Borax}$$

Material	Calculation Formula	Moles	Oxides in Formula / Moles in Formula	Na_2O .3	PbO .4	ZnO .2	BaO .1	B_2O_3 .35	Al_2O_3 .2	SiO_2 3.4
Borax	$Na_2O \cdot 2B_2O_3$	.175		.175				.35		
Soda Ash	Na_2O	.125		.125						
White Lead	PbO	.4			.4					
Zinc Oxide	ZnO	.2				.2				
Barium Carbonate	BaO	.1					.1			
Clay	$Al_2O_3 \cdot 2SiO_2$	.2							.2	.4
Flint	SiO_2	3.0								3.0
			Total	.3	.4	.2	.1	.35	.2	3.4

Material	Moles	X	Equivalent Weight	=	Weight Factor	X	Key	=	% Batch
Borax	.175	x	381	=	66.675	x	.2217	=	14.782
Soda Ash	.125	x	106	=	13.250	x	.2217	=	2.938
White Lead	.4	x	259	=	103.600	x	.2217	=	22.968
Zinc Oxide	.2	x	81	=	16.200	x	.2217	=	3.592
Barium Carbonate	.1	x	197	=	19.700	x	.2217	=	4.367
Clay	.2	x	258	=	51.600	x	.2217	=	11.440
Flint	3.0	x	60	=	180.000	x	.2217	=	39.906
				100 ÷ 451.025 = .2217					99.993

Problem F

$$\frac{.27\ Na_2O}{.49\ Na_2O} = .551 \quad Kona\ F\text{-}4$$

Material	Calculation Formula	Moles	Oxides in Formula / Moles in Formula	Na₂O	K₂O	CaO	ZnO	BaO	Al₂O₃	SiO₂
				.27	.17	.24	.15	.17	.56	4.60
Kona F-4	K₂O.31Al₂O₃1.01SiO₂5.56 Na₂O.49 CaO.20	.55		.27	.17	.11			.56	3.06
Whiting	CaO	.13				.13				
Zinc Oxide	ZnO	.15					.15			
Barium Carbonate	BaO	.17						.17		
Flint	SiO₂	1.54								1.54
			Total	.27	.17	.24	.15	.17	.56	4.60

Material	Moles	X	Equivalent Weight	=	Weight Factor	X	Key	=	% Batch
Kona F-4	.55	x	508	=	279.40	x	.2323	=	64.905
Whiting	.13	x	100	=	13.00	x	.2323	=	3.020
Zinc Oxide	.15	x	81	=	12.15	x	.2323	=	2.822
Barium Carbonate	.17	x	197	=	33.49	x	.2323	=	7.780
Flint	1.54	x	60	=	92.40	x	.2323	=	21.465
				100 ÷ 430.44 = .2323					99.992

Problem G

Material	Batch	÷	Equivalent Weight	=	Mole Factor
White Lead (PbO)	46.4	÷	259	=	.179
Whiting (CaO)	9.3	÷	100	=	.093
Zinc Oxide (ZnO)	2.4	÷	81	=	.030
Clay ($Al_2O_3 \cdot 2SiO_2$)	19.4	÷	258	=	.075
Flint (SiO_2)	22.5	÷	60	=	.375

PbO	.179	Al_2O_3	.075	SiO_2	.375
CaO	.093				+.150
ZnO	.030				.525

$1 \div .302 = 3.311$ Key

PbO	.179	x	3.311	=	.593
CaO	.093	x	3.311	=	.308
ZnO	.030	x	3.311	=	.099
Al_2O_3	.075	x	3.311	=	.248
SiO_2	.525	x	3.311	=	1.738

PbO	.59	Al_2O_3	.25	SiO_2	1.74
CaO	.31				
ZnO	.10				

Problem H

Material	Batch	Equivalent Weight	=	Mole Factor
Nepheline Syenite	45.3	432	=	.105
Whiting	9.7	100	=	.097
Barium Carbonate	23.2	197	=	.118
Zinc Oxide	8.8	81	=	.109
Clay	13.0	258	=	.050

Material	Calculation Formula	Moles	Oxides in Formula	Na$_2$O	K$_2$O	CaO	BaO	ZnO	Al$_2$O$_3$	SiO$_2$
Nepheline Syenite	Na$_2$O.74Al$_2$O$_3$.99SiO$_2$4.36 K$_2$O.24 CaO.02	.105		.078	.025	.002			.104	.458
Whiting	CaO	.097				.097				
Barium Carbonate	BaO	.118					.118			
Zinc Oxide	ZnO	.109						.109		
Clay	Al$_2$O$_3$•2SiO$_2$	.050							.050	.100
			Total	.078	.025	.099	.118	.109	.154	.558

Na$_2$O   .078   Al$_2$O$_3$ .154   SiO$_2$ .558
K$_2$O   .025
CaO   .099
BaO   .118
ZnO   .109
     1 ÷ .429 = 2.331   Key

Na$_2$O	.078	x	2.331	=	.182
K$_2$O	.025	x	2.331	=	.059
CaO	.099	x	2.331	=	.231
BaO	.118	x	2.331	=	.275
ZnO	.109	x	2.331	=	.254
Al$_2$O$_3$	.154	x	2.331	=	.359
SiO$_2$	.558	x	2.331	=	1.301

Na$_2$O   .18   Al$_2$O$_3$ .36   SiO$_2$ 1.30
K$_2$O   .06
CaO   .23
BaO   .28
ZnO   .25

Problem I

Material	Percentage	÷	Equivalent Weight	=	Mole Factor	X	Key	=	Formula
SiO_2	66.3	÷	60	=	1.105	x	5.6497	=	6.24
Al_2O_3	18.4	÷	102	=	.180	x	5.6497	=	1.02
CaO	.4	÷	56	=	.007	x	5.6497	=	.040
Na_2O	2.7	÷	62	=	.044	x	5.6497	=	.249
K_2O	11.8	÷	94	=	.126	x	5.6497	=	.712
					$1 ÷ .177 = 5.6497$				1.001

Material	Moles	X	Equivalent Weight	=	Weight Factor
K_2O	.71	x	94	=	66.74
Na_2O	.25	x	62	=	15.50
CaO	.04	x	56	=	2.24
Al_2O_3	1.02	x	102	=	104.04
SiO_2	6.24	x	60	=	374.40
					562.92

K_2O	.71	Al_2O_3 1.02	SiO_2	6.24
Na_2O	.25			
CaO	.04			

Equivalent Weight   563

Problem J

Material	Percentage	÷	Equivalent Weight	=	Mole Factor	X	Key	=	Formula
SiO_2	67.1	÷	60	=	1.118	x	5.3767	=	6.010
Al_2O_3	19.1	÷	102	=	.187	x	5.376	=	1.005
CaO	.94	÷	56	=	.017	x	5.376	=	.091
Na_2O	6.56	÷	62	=	.106	x	5.376	=	.570
K_2O	5.91	÷	94	=	.063	x	5.376	=	.339
					$1 ÷ .186 = 5.376$				1.000

Material	Moles	X	Equivalent Weight	=	Weight Factor
K_2O	.34	x	94	=	31.96
Na_2O	.57	x	62	=	35.34
CaO	.09	x	56	=	5.04
Al_2O_3	1.01	x	102	=	103.02
SiO_2	6.01	x	60	=	360.60
					535.96

K_2O .34 Al_2O_3 1.01 SiO_2 6.01
Na_2O .57
CaO .09

Equivalent Weight 536

Appendix F Manufacturers List

Clay Mixers

Bluebird Manufacturing
c/o Judson Pottery
100 Gregory Rd.
Ft. Collins, Colorado 80521

Kilns

A.D. Alpine, Inc.
3051 Fujita Street
Torrance, California 90505

MSI Industries, Inc.
3800 Race St.
Denver, Colorado 80205

Ipsen Industries
Box 6266
Rockford, Illinois 61125

Unique Kilns, HED Industries, Inc.
Box 176
Pennington, New Jersey

L & L Manufacturing Company
142 Conchester Rd.
Twin Oaks, Pennsylvania 19016

Wheels

Robert Brent Company
128 Mill St.
Healdsburg, California 95448

Shimpo Industries Ltd.
c/o Shimpo-West
Box 2315
La Puente, California 91746

Hand Tools

Kemper Manufacturing Company
Box 545
Chino, California 91710

Photo Resist Process

Picceramic
817 Ethel Place
Vestal, New York 13850

Overglaze

Ceramic Color and Chemical
   Manufacturing Company
Box 297
New Brighton, Pennsylvania 15066

Luster Glaze

Med-Mar Metals
Box 78313
Los Angeles, California 90016

Decals

CeramiCorner Inc.
Box 516
Azusa, California 91702

Miscellaneous

American Art Clay
4717 West Sixteenth St.
Indianapolis, Indiana 46222

Appendix G Temperature Equivalents for Orton Standard Pyrometric Cones

Cone Number	Large Cones		Small Cones	
	¹60°C	108°F	300°C	540°F
022	585°C	1085°F	630°C	1165°F
021	602	1116	643	1189
020	625	1157	666	1231
019	668	1234	723	1333
018	696	1285	752	1386
017	727	1341	784	1443
016	764	1407	825	1517
015	790	1454	843	1549
014	834	1533	870	1596
013	869	1596	880	1615
012	876	1609	900	1650
011	886	1627	915	1680
†010	887	1629	919	1686
09	915	1679	955	1751
08	945	1733	983	1801
07	973	1783	1008	1846
06	991	1816	1023	1873
05	1031	1888	1062	1944
04	1050	1922	1098	2008
03	1086	1987	1131	2068
02	1101	2014	1148	2098
01	1117	2043	1178	2152
1	1136	2077	1179	2154
2	1142	2088	1185	2165
3	1152	2106	1196	2185
4	1168	2134	1209	2208
5	1177	2151	1221	2230
6	1201	2194	1255	2291
7	1215	2219	1264	2307
8	1236	2257	1300	2372
9	1260	2300	1317	2403
10	1285	2345	1330	2426
11	1294	2361	1336	2437
12	1306	2383	1355	2471
13	1321	2410	——	——
14	1388	2530	——	——
15	1424	2595	——	——

† Iron-free (white) are made in numbers 010 to 3. The iron-free cones have the same deformation temperatures as the red equivalents when fired at a rate of 60 Centigrade degrees per hour in air.

Notes:

1. The temperature equivalents in this table apply only to Orton Standard Pyrometric Cones, *when heated at the rates indicated, in an air atmosphere.*

2. Temperature Equivalents are given in degrees Centigrade (°C.) and the corresponding degrees Fahrenheit (°F.). The rates of heating shown at the head of each column of temperature equivalents were maintained during the last several hundred degrees of temperature rise.

3. The temperature equivalents were determined at the National Bureau of Standards by H. P. Beerman (see Journal of the American Ceramic Society, Vol. 39, 1956).

4. The temperature equivalents are not necessarily those at which cones will deform under firing conditions different from those under which the calibrating determinations were made. For more detailed technical data, please write the Orton Foundation.

5. Conversion Factors: *Centigrade to Fahrenheit* N x 9 ÷ 5 + 32; *Fahrenheit to Centigrade* N - 32 x 5 ÷ 9.

Courtesy: The Edward Orton Jr. Ceramic Foundation, 1445 Summit Street, Columbus, Ohio 43201

Index